James Nisbet and Company

The holy childhood

Conversations on the earliest portion of the gospel narrative

James Nisbet and Company

The holy childhood
Conversations on the earliest portion of the gospel narrative

ISBN/EAN: 9783741163708

Manufactured in Europe, USA, Canada, Australia, Japa

Cover: Foto ©Lupo / pixelio.de

Manufactured and distributed by brebook publishing software (www.brebook.com)

James Nisbet and Company

The holy childhood

THE HOLY CHILDHOOD.

MOONLIGHT.

THE
HOLY CHILDHOOD.

*CONVERSATIONS ON THE EARLIEST
PORTION OF THE GOSPEL
NARRATIVE.*

"Consider Him."

LONDON:
JAMES NISBET & CO., 21 BERNERS STREET.
MDCCCLXXVII.

PREFACE.

THIS book is published in the hope that to some Mothers, or other Teachers, it may afford a little aid in imparting Biblical instruction; varying, at least for fifteen mornings, the method, too apt to stiffen into routine, of daily Bible readings. It is therefore intended rather to be read to children, than to be read by them.

It assumes that they are already acquainted with the outline of the Gospel history, and with that of the books of Genesis and Exodus. Also that they have received some instruction in the elements of the Christian faith.

For these reasons the Conversations will hardly be found suitable for very young children, and probably even for older ones it will be necessary here and there to explain a word.

It is earnestly desired by the Writer, that in every instance the Scripture references may be sought out by the children themselves.

CONTENTS.

	PAGE
INTRODUCTION	1
CHAP.	
I. GOD IS	9
II. THE WORD	23
III. "YES"	39
IV. ZACHARIAS AND ELIZABETH	58
V. MARY	72
VI. GOOD NEWS	87
VII. CIRCUMCISION	102
VIII. THE PRESENTATION IN THE TEMPLE	120
IX. THE STAR IN THE EAST	141
X. "THE KING OF THE JEWS"	159
XI. THE PASSOVER	175

CHAP.	PAGE
XII. GOD'S HOLY CHILD AT JERUSALEM . . .	193
XIII. GOD'S HOLY CHILD AT NAZARETH . . .	213
XIV. GROWTH	232
XV. GOD'S WITNESSES	251
XVI. CONCLUSION—OUR TEACHER . . .	275
APPENDIX	280

THE HOLY CHILDHOOD.

INTRODUCTION.

THIS is not a story-book. I want all the children who may read it to understand that quite plainly at first, and then they can't say afterwards that they were taken in by the look of it.

There is, indeed, a Story partly told in it, which is worth all other stories put together, but that is one you all know, or at least, think you know quite well, for it is only the Story of how JESUS came down to this world of ours, and lived, and suffered, and died here for us.

Only!—But do you think we shall ever find another story as wonderful, or as beautiful, or one that can do us as much good? I am quite sure we never shall; and so before we leave it for new story-books, would it not be a good plan to try if we can't get more out of this old one than we have ever done before?

If we do want to please God, and ask Him—*really meaning it*—to teach us to understand His Book, we shall get something worth having out of it, I can promise you that! Something that we can always keep, and that will always make us happy, long, long after we have forgotten all our other story-books, and that we shall really want more and more, and shall never get tired of.

Other story-books are often very nice and very amusing, and nearly everybody likes being amused—at all events you and I do—only you see there are so many people ready and waiting to amuse us, and such heaps of funny books written, that we might sit and read them all our whole lives and never stop, and then we shouldn't get half through them. So I am sure that as life is so short (though you mayn't have found that out yet), and there is so much real work that must be done in it, that it is better to try and do a little towards helping people to know more about God, and about what He has done to make us happy for ever, than just to help them to "pass away the time," as idle people say. There is some sense in that, don't you think there is? And that is why I am not just now writing a story-book.

So please remember that this book is not written to amuse you; and that Mr. and Mrs. Hillyard and their children are only put in to make the Bible Story seem more real when ordinary children like yourselves talk about it, and to make you remember it better. However, we will suppose that they lived most part of the year in a house in the country, and that the family consisted of father, mother, and four children—Myles, who was fifteen, and just now spending his summer holidays at home; Phyllis, who was a year or two younger; Jack, who was between eight and nine; and little Elsie, who was only seven.

There was nothing very remarkable about any of them. They were not particularly beautiful, neither were they ugly. They were not extraordinarily clever, nor were they at all stupid. They were glad enough to know things, though like most of us, they didn't care about the trouble of learning; and I am afraid they liked reading story-books better than lessons a very great deal; and certainly they liked running about out of doors with their dogs, and looking after all their other animals, and swinging, and riding, and climbing trees, and rowing on the river, and fishing, better than either. That was the sort of children they were. Luckily for them, their parents were fond of the same kind of things, when they had time to amuse themselves; and they used to have great fun all together, particularly in the holidays, when Myles was at home. Mr. and Mrs. Hillyard thought that childhood, like colthood, and lambhood, and puppyhood, and kittenhood, was the time when God meant young creatures to play and be merry, and have what our American cousins call a "good time." So a "good time" these children had and no mistake!

Will it surprise any other children who may have this book read to them, to hear that two of them certainly, and their mother hoped and believed all of them, really wanted to be good as well as happy, and to please God more than to please themselves? Therefore, though they didn't much like most of their lessons, they used to try and do them well. I don't see why that need be so very surprising. You see their mother had always taught them that our Father in Heaven loved them, and didn't, and couldn't grudge them any good thing—and that He had proved His Love to them in a way there could be no mistaking, by giving to die, for them, His " One Son, His Well-beloved ; " and I think they really felt that after that the least they could do was to try and please Him, and they *did* try, and taking it altogether, succeeded in doing many little things for Him, though they didn't say anything about it.

I am afraid they were often very naughty, all of them, and they liked uncommonly to get their own way, as you and I do too, perhaps. But still they did sometimes give up their wills to God, though it was not always easy, and they could not have done it but for Him helping them.

Every morning they read the Bible with their mother. Their other lessons, Phyllis and Jack, at least, mostly did with their governess. They were very fond of her, and it was not *her* fault that they didn't enjoy them more. But their Bible lesson their mother always gave them herself, and sometimes when their father was able, he came and read with them too. It was always a pleasant time, for they were not a bit afraid of their parents, and used to say just what they really thought about things. And then, for another thing, it was always short, so that they had hardly time to get tired and fidgety.

They really liked learning about God. They did not, of course, understand a great deal of the Bible, but they felt that what they did understand was somehow more a real thing to them than their other lessons. It was about things which they knew and felt concerned *them*—their very own selves—in a way that the history of Rome, and even of England, didn't do, far less arithmetic, and geography, and French and Latin grammar. And though this realness had sometimes frightened them, and made them feel it was an awful thing to be so closely connected with God, yet it was perhaps this very fear that had made them bent on finding out exactly what it was they had to do to be safe and happy with Him for ever; and it was made very plain to them that they had not got to do anything at all for *that*, as God Himself had done it all long ago, and all they had to do was to say "Yes" to Him, really and truly,—meaning it. Does anybody not understand this, and wonder what it could be they had to say "yes" to? Perhaps Mrs. Hillyard may explain that presently.

We will follow them through fifteen of their Readings—through just the very earliest part of the Gospel history, but *they* went steadily on to the end of it, just as they had been through Genesis, and as the elder ones had already been through the whole Bible; because regular reading, straight on, was the plan their parents thought the best, and the most profitable, though on Sundays it had generally been their habit particularly to study some special subject, wherever in the Bible it might be traced.

A Tree stands on a mountain,
  And golden fruit it yields
All through the snows of winter,
  And when flowers are in the fields.
And late and early many come
  To seek the shining gold ;
And still they shake it from the Tree,
  As they have done of old.

None leave it empty-handed,
  Yet the Tree is never bare ;
The more the fruit is gathered,
  The more is growing there.
For the fruit is given by God in Heaven
  In love and mercy free,
That great and small it may comfort all,
  And the Bible is that Tree.

CHAPTER I.
GOD IS.

HEB. XI. 6; EXOD. III. 13-15.

NE summer's morning Mrs. Hillyard's two younger children came running into her sitting-room for their usual Bible reading, and settled themselves side by side—a very bright little pair—on the ottoman in the window.

Myles and Phyllis were there already. It was Myles' first day at home these holidays, and his mother and sister had been busy showing him some new photographs that had been taken of the house during his absence. It was a nice house—square and solid-looking outside, and thoroughly comfortable within. The room where they had met for their reading was a particularly cheerful one, with a south-east aspect, so that if the sun shone at all in the mornings, it shone full into that room, unless the awning had been put up outside.

"Well, Mother, what are we to read to-day?" asked Jack, with a good deal of suppressed elation at the thoughts of "doing lessons with Myles;" for Myles was a person of very great importance and dignity in the eyes of his younger brother.

"We were talking it over after breakfast," replied Mrs. Hillyard, "and we think it will be best to begin the gospels, putting them all together as far as we can do so, into one story. And what a Story that is! The 'old old Story' of the Life, and Death, and Resurrection, and Ascension of our Blessed Lord. May He Himself help us—even you two flighty little things—to read and hear It gravely, and to remember what a solemn responsibility it is, and what a wonderful privilege too to be allowed to read that Story, and to learn about Him."

"Yes, of course, Mumsey," said Jack, "only we do know a great deal about Jesus, and we did so want to hear what happened to Moses and the children of Israel in the wilderness. Mayn't we finish that first?"

"No, dear. I told you that they did arrive in Canaan after their forty years' wanderings—at least their children did—for all the Israelites that left Egypt died in the wilderness except Joshua and Caleb. You have been right through Genesis, and Exodus, as far as chapter xxi., and now I think it is quite time you read carefully through the gospels."

"Are Myles and Phyllis to read with us?" asked little Elsie.

"Yes, of course we are," said Phyllis, answering for herself and brother.

"But," said Jack, "you two old ones have read the four gospels through and through, and know lots of them off by heart."

"Ah, but *Myles* doesn't think 'he knows a great deal about Jesus,'" observed Mrs. Hillyard. "Do you, Myles?"

"No," said Myles gravely; "in one way I seem to know next to nothing about Him, but in another way, if you understand me, Mother, I think we all know too much."

"I quite understand you, dear, only I don't think the fault lies in our knowing too much about Christ; but that the knowledge has not brought forth more fruit in our lives. And why do you think that is, Myles? It is an important question."

"Well, I suppose it is partly that we read it off too much like a bit of history, and have done with it."

"Yes, I think so," said Mrs. Hillyard, "and I am so glad you have warned us before we began, not to read the story of His Blessed Life in that heartless way. We all need the warning, particularly, perhaps, the little ones, who are so apt to think of their Bible reading as 'lessons. It is 'lessons' indeed in one sense, but do remember, darlings, that our Lord Jesus Christ is our own real Friend and Saviour, and not some one who once lived a long way off, and who lives ever so much farther off now that He is in Heaven. The sort of knowledge we want first of all about Him is that He is a Real Person now, and that He is here, and sees us, and hears us, and above all that He loves us very much more than I love you. Till we know Him a little in that way, it can hardly do us any good to know the facts of His Life and Death in Palestine."

"No, Mother—that's just it," said Phyllis; "only you know it *is* hard always to feel like that about a Person we have never seen."

"Hard!" exclaimed her mother, "it is impossible without faith. But that is just what faith is for. Our whole walk here must be by faith—'as seeing Him Who is invisible.' We don't *see* any of the spiritual things we talk about. And so before we begin our reading this morning let us pray that God would 'increase our faith,' and Himself teach us in His Word by the Holy Ghost."

After a few words of prayer Mrs. Hillyard asked Jack to find Heb. xi. 6, and when he had read the verse aloud she said—

"I daresay you and Elsie wonder why we should begin with that text this morning; but it is always well to be quite sure that we understand the very beginning of any subject we want to learn about, particularly religion, and that passage seems to me to be text number one in the whole Bible. If we spend all our time over it this morning it won't matter. We can begin St. John to-morrow, and shall lose nothing by putting it off."

"What—and have no story at all to-day?" asked Elsie.

"I don't know, darling; perhaps I may tell you a story—we shall see. But now you *think*, little one, and tell me—what does this verse tell us is the first thing any one must do before he can come to God? I will read it to you slowly, 'Without faith it is impossible to please God; for he that cometh to God must believe that HE IS'—well?"

"He 'must believe that He is,'" answered Elsie.

"Yes, and what does that mean? Can you tell me, Jack?"

"Why, I suppose it only means that, of course, you couldn't come to anybody unless you believed there was such a person."

"Quite so, that is the meaning of it; and as we can't please God, or be happy ourselves, unless we have made a right beginning, we should make quite sure that we do 'believe that HE IS.'"

"But of course we believe that," said Jack.

"I am afraid it is not 'of course' at all," answered his mother. "Depend upon it, many people are really infidels who are called Christians."

"What are infidels, Mumsey?" asked little Elsie.

"An infidel merely means a person who doesn't believe, though the name is generally given only to people who say in so many words that they do not believe in God, or Christ, or the Bible. But we may be practically infidels though we don't know it. We may go to church, and repeat the Creed, and think we believe it all, but if we don't act as if we did, it is no use our saying so, and our actions tell a truer tale than our words."

"How do you mean, Mother?" asked Phyllis.

"Well, I mean this, that if people really believed in God they could hardly go on as they do. For instance, thousands of men, and women, and children will quietly say day by day, or at any rate, Sunday by Sunday, 'Thy Kingdom come,' knowing, if they think about the meaning of the words at all, that the Lord's Coming would be the most terrible and overwhelming calamity that could befall them. Do you think they could offer such a prayer as that if they believed they were saying it to a Real Person Who might take them at their word?"

"No," said Myles, "not if they thought what they were saying, but then we often don't think."

"True, but I cannot say I see much difference between such habitual thoughtlessness and infidelity. Then, again, no one with any real belief in God would, I think, dare to take His Name in vain. I will give you another instance—I heard a boy the other day, shouting out at the very top of his voice, whilst his companions were playing, a hymn which I suppose had been given him to learn. He was evidently doing it for fun, and meant no harm by it, but the words were the most solemn that could be uttered, and were about the Sufferings and Death of our Lord Jesus Christ; and as I heard them, though the irreverence and heartlessness shocked me so, almost my first thought was,—'there is an infidel—at this moment, at any rate, as daring an infidel as ever lived.' If he had really believed in a God Who actually saw and heard him, do you think he could have made game of such a hymn?"

"Of course, he couldn't," said Jack.

"And so, in every act of irreverence," continued Mrs. Hillyard, "I do think it is more or less of unbelief that is at the bottom of it. When people sit comfortably in their pews whilst prayer is being offered to God, or when children throw Bibles carelessly about, and jabber over their texts and hymns—I don't want to judge them—but it does *seem* as if they had not yet got hold of the very first beginning of all true religion—the great fact that GOD IS."

"And I suppose," said Phyllis, "that when we do any wrong things, it is because we forget that."

"No doubt, just because God is 'Invisible.' If He were not, it would make the whole difference in our conduct. It is all from want of faith that we commit sin. I told Elsie that perhaps I would tell her a story, and so I will, and it is a true one too:—

"I remember when I was a little girl about ten years old, that several friends had come to play with me. It was a winter's evening, and some of us had been locked up in a room by

B

the rest. I forget exactly why—they were preparing some surprise for us I think, which we were not to see till it was all completed. I got tired of being shut up in the dark, and besides was dying of curiosity to see what was going on. Johnny Irons, the clergyman's son, a boy of my own age, was with me, besides one or two more. The others were just outside the door, and we begged them in vain to let us out.

"At last I whispered to my little fellow-prisoner—'Johnny, do ask them to let me out just for a minute. Say I really must run and get a pocket-handkerchief.'

"But Johnny answered, 'No, I should be afraid to say that.'

"'Afraid!' I said. 'What should you be afraid of?'

"'Why, it would be wrong,' he said, 'it wouldn't be true.' Johnny had not forgotten, you see, as I had, that GOD IS; and as long as I live I shall remember the awe with which those words impressed me. In the midst of our game I felt myself suddenly to be in the very presence of God. It was because he was a child like myself that it struck me so: so let that show you, dears, that you have an influence with your own generation now, that you will most likely never have again; and see you use it faithfully. Johnny has been a clergyman now for many years himself, and I hope has impressed his parishioners with as real a sense of God's Presence, as he did me in that dark room when he was ten years old.

"And now, Jack, tell me—What was the first message God sent to the Israelites in Egypt, when He was come down to deliver them?"

"I forget," answered Jack.

"Do you remember, Phyllis? It is not long since you all read it."

"No, I am afraid I don't," Phyllis was forced to confess also.

"Well, then, read the passage; you will find it in Exodus iii. 13–15. I am sorry you all have such short memories."

Phyllis then read—"And Moses said unto God, Behold, when I come unto the children of Israel, and shall say unto them, The God of your fathers hath sent me unto you; and they shall say to me, What is His Name? what shall I say unto them? And God said unto Moses,

I AM THAT I AM: and He said, Thus shalt thou say unto the children of Israel, I AM hath sent me unto you."

"Now," said Mrs. Hillyard, "I think even little Elsie can tell me what Name God gave Himself, when He sent this first message to His people?"

"I suppose you mean 'I AM,'" answered Elsie, "but it seems a very odd name."

"Now I shall ask Myles a question—Why did the Lord so call Himself at that time?"

"I never thought of it before," said Myles, "but after what you have said about the real belief that 'HE IS' coming first, I suppose that was the lesson God had first to teach them. Most likely they had been so long in slavery that they had quite forgotten Him."

"Yes, I have no doubt they had been living without any knowledge of God's existence. I mean practical knowledge. Perhaps they could hardly have forgotten what their fathers must have told them about Him, but to *them* He was *nothing*. And so before God taught them anything *about* Himself, He sent them word—'I AM.' He didn't tell them what He was—that

He was Good, and Wise, and Powerful: but there really was such a PERSON as Himself Who was about to have dealings with them. And just in the same way, before He can have any dealings with us now, He has to bring the great fact of His Existence home to our hearts and consciences. Sometimes this frightens us very much when we first begin to feel that it is all true—that there really is a Great GOD Whose Eyes are never off us, and Who hears every word we say. And if we feel frightened at the thought of God, Elsie, what must we do? We can't run away from Him, you know; and He really does see us, and knows all the naughty things we do, and say, and think; and He hates them, and is always angry at sin."

Elsie said nothing, but hung down her head.

"Well, darling, I will tell you what we must do—we must run *to* Him—and how do you think He will receive us?"

"As Jesus did the little children, I think," answered Phyllis—" He took them in His Arms, laid His Hands on them, and blessed them."

"Yes, that is it," said Mrs. Hillyard; "and so you see there is nothing that need really frighten us about God, unless we keep away from Him, for His Love is as real as Himself. To come to Him as you would come to me—knowing that I am your mother, and that I love you—is all you have to do to be quite safe for ever. But how is it, Jack, that we poor sinners may do that?"

"Because Jesus died."

"Yes, thank God He did! And now, that will be enough Bible reading for this morning—and you can run out and dig me up those ferns."

O God, give us such a faith in Thee as shall compel us diligently to seek Thee, and reward us, as Thou hast promised, above all that we can ask or think, for the sake of Thy Son, our Saviour, Jesus Christ. Amen.

My Father, make Thyself to me
A living, bright Reality;
More present to faith's vision keen
Than any outward object seen;
More dear, more intimately nigh,
Than e'en the sweetest earthly tie!

CHAPTER II.*

THE WORD.

JOHN I. 1-5, 9-11.

EXT morning, when the little party again met for their Bible reading, Mrs. Hillyard said that St. John being the Evangelist that went the farthest back in the Story of the Gospel, it would be best to begin with his book; and so, after asking in a short prayer for God's teaching and blessing, she read aloud the verses of St. John's Gospel, above referred to.

She then asked Phyllis, "Who is 'the Word' here spoken of?"

Phyllis. Jesus Christ.

Mrs. Hillyard. Why is He called "the Word"?

Ph. I don't think I quite know, Mother.

---

* It might be well to abridge, if not to omit, this chapter and the next, in reading to younger children.

Mrs. H. What are words for, Jack?

Jack. Words—what are they for? Why, we couldn't talk without them; at least we could make noises, but no one would know what we meant without words.

Mrs. H. Quite right, Jack. The use of words then is to express our thoughts. Now, Jesus is called "the Word" because He expressed God's Thoughts. He came to let the world know that God loved men. Not only the Jews, but everybody. Before Jesus came, nobody knew that "God is Love." The Jews knew that He had loved *them*, but for several hundred years they had felt more of His judgments than His love, and they knew He was very angry with them for their sins. The rest of the world knew nothing whatever about His love, though He had always loved them. They could know if they noticed the things that God had made, that He was very powerful,[*] but the outward creation could never have shown them that He was Love. Certainly He did them good,[†] giving them sunshine, and rain, and fruitful seasons; and making them happy some-

---

[*] Rom. i. 20.   [†] Acts xiv. 17.

times by His gifts; but to set against that, think of all the storms, and droughts, and famines, and pestilences that they suffered from, too. These things told such a different story that they could never find out God's Character from what they saw around them. They didn't know, as we do, that it was sin that brought all this evil into the world, so they couldn't understand it at all; and though their own hearts* and consciences might have told them that He was Good, yet that seemed so contradicted by all the misery they saw and felt, that they could have no notion of either His Love or His Justice till He sent His Son. We should be in just the same darkness now, if it were not for the Bible, telling us about Jesus. But now we know that "God so loved the world, that He gave His only-begotten Son, that whosoever believeth in Him should not perish, but have everlasting life." And that wonderful Gift—God's own Son—we know to be the measure of His Love to us.

Ph. I think I quite see now, Mother, why Jesus is called "the Word."

---

* Gen. i. 27; Rom. ii. 15; Acts xvii. 29.

Mrs. H. I am glad of that, dear child. But now I must try to explain, as far as I can, what these verses mean. You know who wrote this book?

J. Yes, St. John.

Mrs. H. And who was he?

J. One of the Apostles.

Mrs. H. Yes. But remember that God Himself wrote it through him. He wrote the whole Bible, though He employed men to write it for Him, and put it into their minds what to say. Only God could have told us about Christ before He came into the world as a Man. Jesus was always with God, for He Himself is God, and therefore He is the Creator of all things. You will see that clearly said in Colossians i. 16, 17. Will you read it, Myles?

Myles. "For by Him were all things created that are in heaven, and that are in earth, visible and invisible; . . all things were created by Him, and for Him: and He is before all things, and by Him all things consist."

Ph. Mother, what does "in the beginning" mean?—In the beginning of what?

Mrs. H. In the beginning of all created

things, I suppose it means—the things mentioned in the verse Myles has just read in Colossians. There is a wonderful passage in the Old Testament, teaching the same truth, that perhaps you have not noticed—Myles and Phyllis, I mean—the little ones, of course, have not. You will find it in the 8th of Proverbs. Will you read it, Phyllis, from the 22d to the 36th verse?

When Phyllis had read these verses, Mrs. Hillyard went on—" There, you see, Christ, speaking as the 'Wisdom of God,' says of Himself that God 'possessed' Him 'in the beginning' of His way, before His works of old. These things are a great deep; but though we cannot understand them, at least we may remember that it was Jesus who made all the beautiful things we see—the same Jesus who was a little Child on earth Himself."

J. But it was God the Father too, wasn't it, Mother?

Mrs. H. Certainly, and the Holy Ghost. All the Three Persons of the Blessed Trinity were engaged in the Work of Creation. Don't you remember how God said, "Let US make man in Our Image, after Our Likeness"?

J. Oh yes, of course, I do now, quite well!

Mrs. H. And so, because He made us in His Own Image and Likeness, we are all His children; and He provided for us with a Father's love. He knew just what we should want; what sort of air we must have to breathe, and what kind of food would be good for us; and He remembered that many of us would need fires to warm us; whilst people in hot countries would like plenty of juicy fruit to quench their thirst. And He even prepared for our need of clothes, and made the flax plants, and cotton trees, and silk-worms, and woolly sheep.

Elsie. Did God really think of all that before He made people!

J. Don't you remember, Elsie, that Mother told us so before, when we were reading Genesis?

Mrs. H. I daresay Elsie doesn't remember everything we talked about then, she was so very little.—And so our Father got the world all ready for His children before He put them into it, and when they were created they found everything they wanted, all ready to hand, as it were. But it had taken God thousands of ages to get the world ready for them. It was not till after all sorts of changes and convulsions in it had taken place, that there could be trees or flowers; or that the coal could be made, or the other minerals that men would require could be forced up to the surface of the earth, so as to be within their reach. And all the long, long time that God was preparing the world for us, He was thinking of us with love and doing it all to make us happy.

E. How wonderfully kind and good of Him!

Mrs. H. Wasn't it! But He was far more loving and thoughtful than that. He knew exactly what we should *like*, as well as what it would be necessary for us to eat, and drink, and wear. He knew what pleasure beautiful sights and sounds would give us, so He provided for our pleasures too, giving us "all things richly to enjoy." So whenever you see any pretty flowers, or leaves, or butterflies, you can think that Jesus made all these things, and meant you to be pleased with them; and when you hear beautiful music, you may remember that *that* is one of His kind Thoughts for you too.

M. I remember so well, Father writing to us from Switzerland, and saying that the mountains and waterfalls, and even the lovely little ferns and mosses gave him ever so much greater pleasure because every one of them showed what some of God's Thoughts were, and that His Ideas of what was beautiful were the same as ours. I know so well what he meant, don't you, Mother?

Mrs. H. Yes, I know quite well: and doesn't it make us feel that though God is so Great and so Holy, yet He is indeed our Father? We seem to feel our family likeness, though we are sinners, when we share in some small measure His Ideas as to what is beautiful.

M. Yes, and it makes Heaven seem more home-like too.

Mrs. H. Quite so, dear.

M. And then, Mother, do you think God provided for what you might call our intellectual pleasure? I mean in reading, and studying science, and that sort of thing?

Mrs. H. I am sure He did. He says His works are "sought out of all them that have pleasure therein," and that "He hath set the world in" our "hearts," though "no man can find out the work that God maketh from the beginning to the end." So that in our researches into natural science, there is always the excitement of making new discoveries, because there ever remains something beyond still undiscovered, and always will be. All these pleasures and interests are abused by men, and are often turned by the devil against God, so that people "worship and serve the creature more than the Creator."

J. Mumsey, do you think God meant to amuse us too?

Mrs. H. Well, dear, you ask me questions I can't answer sometimes. He hasn't told us that, but I believe certainly He did, or He would not have made kittens, and puppies, and monkeys so very funny as they are. And I am sure He meant us to be fond of animals, and fitted some of them, like dogs and horses, to be our companions. But all this would not have been enough for us. The need of our hearts and affections had to be more fully provided for. So what did God give Adam besides all these things?

Ph. Do you mean Eve, Mother?

Mrs. H. Yes; He saw that it was "not good for man to be alone," so He gave Adam a wife, and He has given us friends and relations to love: but no worldly goods, and no pretty things, and no knowledge, and no friends even are enough to satisfy our hearts, and make us really happy; and so God gave us Himself—and to know and love Him is what alone can supply all our needs, and fully satisfy us.

But I have said nothing yet about the Greatest Provision of our Father's Love—about That which puts all His other Loving Kindnesses into the shade. I have kept That for the last. "Before the foundation of the world," God had also provided for a great and terrible need of ours, which He foresaw would arise—our greatest need of all—brought about by an evil which nothing short of such inconceivable Love as His could have met. What was that, Jack?

J. Sin.

Mrs. H. Yes, and what was "God's remedy for sin"?

E. Jesus.

Mrs. H. Yes. I am so glad you understood

THE WORD.

me, little one. It is Jesus—Jesus only. "God provided Himself a Lamb for a burnt-offering," "the Lamb slain before the foundation of the world." And so "in the fulness of time" (that means when the right time came) Jesus, the Word, came down here to live as a poor man, and to suffer and die. Elsie said just now how wonderfully good God has been to us, and so indeed He has. But oh! my darlings, let us think, as far as we can, what was "the manner of love" that led Him to give up His Son! The work of creation, after all, only cost Him so many thoughts—He said, "Let there be light, and there was light:"—but what did the Sacrifice of Jesus cost Him? That is a mystery we may never know, though we do know that all His other gifts put together are nothing compared to this Gift. But God knew that only by giving up Jesus to die, He could save us from the power of sin and death. "In Him was life; and the life was the light of men." Tell me, Phyllis, what is "the wages of sin"?

Ph. Death.

Mrs. H. Yes, "by sin came death" (to mankind), and by sin came darkness too—spiritual darkness, I mean—a darkness that shut out God from His creatures, and separated them from Him. And so the only cure for this poor world over which the prince of darkness reigned, was that Jesus in Whom alone is Life and Light, should come down "to bring Life and Immortality to light through the Gospel;" and by revealing God to man again, and reconciling sinners to God, should give Eternal Life to all who would believe in Him.

M. Only then they wouldn't believe in Him !

Mrs. H. No, indeed ! when He came, hardly anybody would listen to Him. People didn't think they were in the dark about God; particularly the Jews who prided themselves on knowing all about Him, because they knew the words of His law, and because they believed a great many absurd stories which their teachers had invented about God, and heaven, and hell, and things that they considered it right and wrong to do. The teaching of Jesus about His Father was much too simple for them—they could not understand it. The light from Heaven would have shown them to be all in the wrong, and great sinners too; whereas they thought themselves wonderfully good, and so they loved the darkness and hated the light.

M. Do you know, Mother, Christ's coming "to His own," and their not receiving Him, always reminds me of those stories about people who have gone away for many years, and have come back again so changed that nobody knew them, or would believe that it was really them. You know what I mean?—though, of course, it is a very poor comparison.

Mrs. H. Oh yes, I see exactly what you mean. Sometimes in these stories, a king has returned to his country and found a usurper reigning on his throne, and his people obeying him, having forgotten their rightful sovereign. Or a husband has come back to his own house, and found that his wife had thought he was dead, and had married some one else. But no such stories can be anything but the faintest picture of this wonderful Story. Here was the King of the whole earth, and not only its King but its Creator, come down to it, and hardly any of His Creatures, and His Subjects, would have anything to say to Him, and mocked at the very thought of His Claims. "He was in the world, and the world was made by Him, and the world knew Him not. He came unto His own, and His own received Him not."

Ph. Does "His own" mean every one, or only the Jews?

Mrs. H. It is true of every one who ever heard of Him, for the whole world is His; but I think it means especially the Jews, because He came as a Jew to be King of Israel. Still it is possible, now, for people to reject Christ— even those who call themselves by His Name —and to say in their hearts, "We will not have this Man to reign over us." I fear there are many who do that, because they know that if they let Him into their hearts, He will reign and be Master there, and they prefer being, as they suppose, their own master, and pleasing themselves, undisturbed. May He keep any of us from the sin of shutting the door against Him!

Our Father Who art in Heaven, we bless Thee that Thou hast made Thyself known to us in the Person of Thy Son, our Saviour, Jesus Christ, and that from His Words, and from His Deeds, by His Life, and by His Death, we may know of a surety that Thou art Love. Sweep away from our hearts every lingering distrust of Thee, so that each of us may come to Thee with boldness in the Name of Jesus, and that so coming we may grow in the knowledge of Thee, and in likeness to Thee, by the power of Thy Blessed Spirit, and to the Glory of Thy Name. Amen.

FOR the beauty of the earth,
   For the beauty of the skies,
For the love which from our birth
   Over and around us lies;
Christ, our God, to Thee we raise
This our hymn of grateful praise.

For the beauty of each hour
   Of the day and of the night,
Hill and vale, and tree and flower,
   Sun and moon and stars of light;
Christ, our God, to Thee we raise
This our hymn of grateful praise.

For the joy of ear and eye,
   For the heart and mind's delight,

For the mystic harmony
   Linking sense to sound and sight ;
Christ, our God, to Thee we raise
This our hymn of grateful praise.

For the joy of human love,
   Brother, sister, parent, child,
Friend on earth, and friends above,
   For all gentle thoughts and mild ;
Christ, our God, to Thee we raise
This our hymn of grateful praise.

For Thyself, best Gift Divine !
   To our race so freely given,
For that great, great Love of Thine—
   Peace on earth, and joy in Heaven ;
Christ, our God, to Thee we raise
This our hymn of grateful praise.
                 The Hymnary.

CHAPTER III.

"YES."

JOHN I. 12, 13, 14.

 YLES brought a friend with him to the reading next morning—a boy about a year younger than himself, called Richard Leigh. He had come over on his bicycle the day before, from his own home which was about eight miles off. He was an odd boy, very quiet and reserved in his manners, though Myles declared with "no end of go in him when his blood was up." In the meantime, however, he appeared not only quiet but unhappy. There was an injured manner about him, and he spoke rather as if he expected, and almost desired, to be contradicted. That was owing, perhaps, to its having been always diligently impressed upon his mind at home, what a very naughty boy he was. Everyone had always told him so, and no doubt there was a good deal of truth in what they said. But yet Myles liked him, and so did Mrs. Hillyard. She felt sorry for him, for she knew he was not happy at home, and, moreover, she had a pretty strong conviction that that was not altogether his own fault.

She was glad when Myles brought him into her room for the Bible reading, but *he* looked anything but glad, poor boy! He had begged Myles to let him off, and had offered to clean his gun for him, and to mend his fishing-rod, and even to do some of his Latin verses if only he would. But Myles had taken no notice of these proposals, and had marched him into his mother's boudoir, with "There you are, old fellow, shut up, and sit down."

The first part of this admonition Richard carefully attended to. He "shut up" like a knife, looking as if he never intended to speak again; and very reluctantly he sat down too, in a distant corner, with a glum expression of countenance when Myles handed him a Bible, and told him to find his place. He thought it very odd, and couldn't make out

the children all seeming quite pleased; and
specially he wondered at Myles, "for he isn't
a muff," he reflected, "nor a humbug, nor a
bit sanctimonious."

Poor boy! his own associations with the
Bible, and with everything that is called
"religion," were far from pleasant; and it is not
too much to say that he thoroughly hated the
whole concern.

Mrs. Hillyard took no notice of his entrance,
beyond kindly suggesting that he should not sit
quite so far away. She then remarked—

"We were reading yesterday about those
who would not receive Jesus. We have a
happier subject to-day, for we shall read that
there were some who did receive Him as the
very One they had been wanting and looking
for; and that in consequence, they were made
wonderfully blest. Let us read these next three
verses—12, 13, 14—

"'But as many as received Him, to them gave
He power to become the sons of God, even to
them that believe on His name: which were
born, not of blood, nor of the will of the flesh,
nor of the will of man, but of God. And the

Word was made flesh, and dwelt among us (and we beheld His glory, the glory as of the only begotten of the Father), full of grace and truth.'

"We will first consider the 12th and 13th verses, and we will consider them with reference to ourselves, for Christ offers Himself to *us*, for *our* acceptance, just as truly as He offered Himself to the Jews in the days when He walked about the streets of Nazareth, and Capernaum, and Jerusalem. And to as many of us as receive Him as the 'Gift of God' He still gives power to become the children of God, in a way in which we never were His children before. Now I have always told you that the very first thing we have to learn about God, when once we 'believe that HE IS,' and that He is GOOD, is the Relationship in which He stands to us all—that He is our Father, and that we are His children. That is the beginning of all right knowledge of either God or ourselves. The fact of our Divine Parentage runs through the whole length and breadth of the Bible—from the first page in which we read that man was made in the Image of God, to the last, where

Christ speaks of Himself as the Root as well as the Off-spring of David."

Myles. Well then, Mother, it does seem strange that in several places it is said that Christians *become* the children of God. There is this one —and then there is that verse in the 8th of Romans—I can't think of it exactly now...

Mrs. Hillyard. Do you mean, "As many as are led by the Spirit of God, they are the sons of God"?

M. Yes, that is it.

Mrs. H. We will consider these passages in a minute, but first, I want you to give me some texts which distinctly say that people who are not believers in Christ are God's children. We will prove that first before we go on.

M. There is that one where Paul tells the Athenians so.*

Mrs. H. Yes, after quoting with approval one of their own poets, as if by doing so to claim the universal brotherhood of humanity with *him*, a *heathen*, he goes on to say, "Forasmuch then as *we are the children of God*," taking it for granted that all are one family, "we ought

---

* Acts xvii. 28, 29.

not to think that the Godhead is like unto gold, or silver, or stone." As much as to say that we have enough, all of us—even heathens—of the remains of the nature in which we were made, to know better than *that*. There *ought* to be a feeling in us that idolatry is degradation. That passage is so plain that perhaps it is waste of time to look for another to prove the point, but I will show you one more which is no less distinct. Look for Malachi ii. 10. Read it, Jack.

Jack. " Have we not all one Father? hath not one God created us? why do we deal treacherously every man against his brother, by profaning the covenant of our fathers?"

Mrs. H. There, you see, the prophet urges the common Relationship of mankind to God, as a plea for honesty and fair dealing between man and man. We will pass on now; but I wished once more to put this very clearly, because the whole of Christianity must be founded on this truth. Our race has a history prior to Christianity, and prior to the fall of man. Christianity is a grand and glorious Remedy,—but still a Remedy; so we can't begin our Religion there. And we must not begin with the fall either, because God does not begin with that when He tells us about the early history of our race. We must always *begin* with *God*, and "measure," as it has been well said, " from the straight, and not from the crooked line." *Then* comes the awful and overwhelming catastrophe which we call the fall,—when Adam and Eve became sinners. What do you think about it, Richard?

Richard. Oh, I am sure I don't know. I thought no one was God's child till he was what they call "converted," at least I have heard that all my life.

Mrs. H. I see, but still you had a feeling that it wasn't true? Your own heart and conscience told you sometimes that you were God's child all the same?

R. Oh, I don't know that they did. I am not so sure that I have a heart, or a conscience either.

Mrs. Hillyard smiled sadly, and answered,

"I am glad you only say you are not sure, for that shows that it was the very feeling in you that I have spoken of, that raised the doubt."

M. But now, Mother, do get on and tell us

what these other texts mean which speak of people *becoming* God's children.

Mrs. H. I will, as far as I understand them. At first, of course, they seem like a contradiction. Phyllis looks as if she had something to say.

Phyllis. I was only thinking that perhaps they merely mean that when people really believe in Jesus, He brings them back to God, and so they get into their right place again, and after that behave like His children, which they did not do before.

J. Like the story Jesus told about the poor boy who ran away from home and lived with the pigs. It was no good his being his father's son so long as he lived like that.

Mrs. H. No, it was not till he came back to his father's arms that he could claim the privileges of a child, which he had forfeited. But still his sins could not alter the fact that he was his father's child, any more than *our* sins can make God *not our* Father, though they may, and do, destroy all the pleasure and happiness of the Relationship. For we are "rebellious children" all of us, and have become "alienated"

from God "by wicked works." That means separated, and so become like strangers. But the Gospel is the Revelation of a Father's Love. God's message to all the poor lost sinners everywhere now is: You are not orphans— you have a Father—a Father against Whom you have heinously sinned, Whose Heart you have deeply grieved, but Who is still yearning over you, still loving you, still looking out for your return; and Who will receive you, if you will only come to Him, with embraces, and with the kisses of His Love. And what is the Way which our Father has appointed for us to come to Him by? I hope you can all tell me that.

E. Jesus.

Mrs. H. Yes, Jesus is the Way to God; for God is so Good that it is impossible He can overlook evil, and take no account of it; and Sin, from which all evil comes, is so bad — so much greater, and worse, really, than it ever seems to us, that the only punishment which could properly meet it, would be so great that if we sinners were to be punished according to that measure, it would be all up with us, and we should be ruined for ever.

God knew that. He knew, as no one else could, what Sin was, but He "so loved the world, that He gave His only-begotten Son, that whosoever believeth in Him should not perish, but have everlasting life."

Jesus died upon the Cross, and that was sufficient for everybody's sins. God came Himself, willingly, to bear our sins, and to die for us. "He was wounded for our transgressions, He was bruised for our iniquities: the chastisement of our peace" (that means the chastisement by which our peace was procured) "was upon Him; and with His stripes we are healed."

And yet He has left us something to do. Every one is not "delivered from the wrath to come" by Christ's Death. What is it then that we have got to do exactly, before we can be reconciled to God?

Ph. Just say "Yes" to Him—that is all, isn't it?

Mrs. H. Thank God! that is all. You could not have answered my question better. But who can say—for fear there should be the least mistake about it—What is it we have to say YES to?

Ph. To Jesus begging us to trust Him.

Mrs. H. Just so—in fact, our Saviour is saying to each of us—" Will you let Me save you now? You have nothing to do but just to trust Me." And it is to that Entreaty we have to say YES. That as far as I understand it is the Gospel of Christ. His " One Sacrifice for sins for ever " is enough to save us, but we to whom the Gospel is preached, must *take* that Salvation for ourselves.

When we have done that, we are saved out and out from hell,* and we have Eternal Life given us to start with. But mind!—I don't say—God forbid!—that we can sin and get off the punishment;† for though we can never now suffer that awful Loss, which can only be the portion of those who are determined to rebel against the light God has given them, and reject the Saviour He has sent, yet He would not be the Loving Father‡ He is, if He did not punish us when we do wrong, nor should we ever wish to get off that punishment, whatever it may be.

But remember that nobody has any right to

---
* Because the death of Jesus was instead of that for us.
† Ps. lxxxix. 30–36.   ‡ Heb. xii. 6.

think that he is a* Christian, or that he is "saved" in any sense at all, if he does not wish to follow Jesus and to please God; for to all believers, that is, to all who really meant it when they said "Yes" to God, is given some of His own Pure and Holy Nature, which loves the Good, and hates the bad. So that if we are in Christ, He also is in us. I hope you all understand it now? it is very, very simple as to our part in it, and that is all that concerns us. And so just to trust Jesus, is to "receive Him," and to those who do "receive Him," what does our passage this morning tell us that He gives?

Ph. " Power to become the sons of God."

Mrs. H. Yes, when by receiving Jesus we are reconciled again to our Father, and He forgives us all our sins, it makes such a complete change in our position, and in our whole lives, that it may well be called being " born again." †

M. You don't think it means more than that, then? Being "born" seems such a strange way of putting it.

---

* Rom. viii. 9.   † John iii. 7; 1 Peter i. 23.

Mrs. H. I certainly do think it means more— I was just going to say so. God actually gives us an Eternal Life then, which we had not before. So that it is truly a " new birth," and He then becomes in a sense He never was before—in a far higher, and grander sense, our Father—the Father of our spirits.* We shall understand this better if we go back to Adam. When God made man, He " breathed into his nostrils the breath of life," or as it is in the Hebrew, " the breath of *lives*," including the full life of body, soul, and spirit. And before Adam sinned God must have made a " Covenant of Life " † with him, ensuring him a never-ending life of happiness. But it was with Adam, *as a sinless man*, that this Covenant was made, and therefore when he fell into sin he lost Eternal Life, and died. Neither he nor any of his children after him could have any claim to it, for they were all sinners. There is therefore

* Heb. xii. 9.
† So at least the whole "Catholic Church" has always affirmed. See Bull's Works, where this subject is entered into at great length, and the mass of Patristic evidence in favour of the tenet collected. In the opinion of the writer it is supported by Scripture evidence, though not expressed in terms.

a necessity, that those who are born in Adam should be born again in Christ. All this is beyond the little ones, indeed it is a subject in which the wisest are very soon out of their depth, but in spite of that, by the Spirit of God, we may all practically understand, because we *feel* the power of the new birth, if we only will "arise and go to our Father," and so try it.

M. And Mother—I tell you what — look here!

Mrs. H. Well, dear, what discovery have you made?

M. Why the parable of the Prodigal Son says that too, though one wouldn't notice it at first. I mean, it seems as if sinners being just brought home again and God receiving them, was not all that the story was meant to teach: for the father doesn't only say his son "was lost and is found," but before that, he said he was "dead and is alive again."

Mrs. H. Exactly. With what beautiful accuracy that is brought in! I am so glad you noticed it. You see we must take the whole story, for I am quite sure our Lord meant it all for us as well as the Jews—and not only bits of it. Some people talk as though the early part were a mistake, and the poor wandering son had never started from the father's house at all, as though that were a mere ornament to the story; whilst others seem to forget the distance he wandered, and appear to imagine that his going off, away from his father, into a far country, was not such a very serious thing after all. My dear children, do beware of both these errors. Remember that God is your Father, but never think lightly of the terrible evil of Sin, which has made such havoc in our world, and which has placed mankind at such a fearful distance from God. Our being His children makes us more guilty, not less so, when we sin against Him.* I hope even the little ones understand this in some measure. Do you think you do, Elsie?

E. Yes, Mumsey—it seems wickeder to be naughty to you and father, than to Ninny or Miss Fürst.

Mrs. H. And it is, darling; for without a

---

* Deut. xxxii. 6; Mal. i. 6.

shadow of a doubt our earthly relationships are meant to teach us about God, and in a faint way they picture our Relationship to Him. I suppose you have heard all this before, Richard?

R. Some of it, but not all. I have heard often enough that people must be converted.

Mrs. H. And that part is true, dear boy. You should be thankful that you have been clearly told that "except you are converted, and become as a little child, you cannot enter into the kingdom of heaven." We must be converted, for till then we cannot really love God; and He is worthy of our affection—don't you think He must be?

R. Yes, if He is anything like what you say. I did sometimes think He was better than people made Him out.

Mrs. H. I fear we have all been guilty of misrepresenting Him, more or less; and indeed He is infinitely better than the best of us could make Him out. He is perfectly Just,* perfectly Loving; † so how can it be anything

---

* Deut. xxxii. 4.   † 1 John iv. 8.

but a blessed privilege to be His Child "by faith in Jesus Christ"? *

R. No, that must be a good thing to be.

Mrs. H. Good! I should think it *was* good! Do you know what it means to be God's Child in Christ? It means to be started on the road to perfection. It means to be as safe,† and as beloved by the ‡ Father as Jesus is, because it is in § Him that we are accepted. We are now become, in a mysterious, but in a perfectly true way, a part ‖ of Jesus, and are beloved by His Father, and our ¶ Father, with a new Love for His Sake: for He bought us by His own Death ** upon the Cross, and thus made peace,†† and reconciliation ‡‡ for us. But we must stop now. Poor little Elsie is getting tired, and Jack too, I am sure. They will be more interested when we come to the earthly life of Jesus, when "the Word was made Flesh, and dwelt among" men, "full of grace and truth." But I thought

---

* Gal. iii. 26.
† John x. 28, 29; Rom. viii. 1, 38, 39.
‡ John xvii. 23; 1 John iv. 17. § Eph. i. 6; Col. ii. 10.
‖ John xvii. 21, 22; Eph. v. 30. ¶ John xx. 17.
** Acts xx. 28. †† Rom. v. 1; Col. i. 20-22.
‡‡ 2 Cor. v. 18-21.

it best to begin before that. Has any one any question to ask before we close?

J. I have! I want to know what "not of blood" means. It seems so odd.

Mrs. H. I think that means that the birth He was speaking of was not a human relationship. The Jews were not to think that they were the children of God in the highest sense, because they were of the family of Abraham.— May God write all the lessons we have learnt to-day in our hearts, and lead us not only to receive the truth *about* Jesus, but to receive HIM. It is that alone that can save us, and He alone, HIMSELF, that can bless us.

O God, whose blessed Son was manifested that He might destroy the works of the devil, and make us the sons of God, and heirs of eternal life; Grant us, we beseech Thee, that, having this hope, we may purify ourselves even as He is pure; that when He shall appear again with power and great glory, we may be made like unto Him in His eternal and glorious kingdom; where with Thee, O Father, and with the Holy Ghost, He liveth and reigneth, ever one God, world without end. Amen.

(*Collect for the 6th Sunday after Epiphany.*)

NOTHING, either great or small,
Nothing, sinner, no ;
JESUS did it, did it all,
Long, long ago.

When He from His lofty Throne
Stooped to do and die,
Everything was fully done,
"'Tis finished," was His cry.

JESUS, I will trust Thee, trust Thee with my soul ;
Guilty, lost, and helpless, Thou canst make me whole.
There is none in heaven or on earth like Thee :
Thou hast died for sinners—therefore, Lord, for me.

Jesus, I may trust Thee, Name of matchless worth,
Spoken by the angel at Thy wondrous birth ;
Written, and for ever, on Thy Cross of shame,
Sinners read and worship, trusting in that Name.

Jesus, I must trust Thee, pondering Thy ways,
Full of love and mercy all Thine earthly days :
Sinners gathered round Thee, lepers sought Thy face,
None too vile or loathsome for a Saviour's grace.

Jesus, I can trust Thee, trust Thy written word,
Though Thy voice of pity I have never heard ;
When Thy Spirit teacheth, to my taste how sweet—
Only may I hearken, sitting at Thy feet.

Jesus, I do trust Thee, trust without a doubt :
" Whosoever cometh, Thou wilt not cast out ; "
Faithful is Thy promise, precious is Thy blood ;
These my soul's salvation, Thou my Saviour God !
      MARY JANE WALKER.

CHAPTER IV.

ZACHARIAS AND ELIZABETH.

LUKE i. 1-23.

RICHARD LEIGH had left the evening before, returning home again upon his bicycle. It has been already remarked that he was an odd boy, which may account for his having departed from his usual dry, cool manners when he said good-bye to Mrs. Hillyard, and having suddenly broken out in rather hasty confusion—Myles being well out of the way—with "Perhaps you'll kiss me?" Mrs. Hillyard did kiss him, with tears in her eyes, but as he was just off then, not a word more was said, and she did not think it necessary to inform her own children of this little incident.

Soon afterwards, however, she sent him an illuminated card as a book-mark for his Bible, and this was the text upon it—" *Wilt thou not from this time cry unto Me, my* FATHER, *Thou art the Guide of my youth?*"

They met next day as usual.

Mrs. Hillyard. We will begin Luke's Gospel this morning, as it will come next in order.

Phyllis. Luke was not one of the Apostles, was he?

Mrs. H. No, dear, it is generally supposed that he was a doctor—the "beloved physician" St. Paul mentions in Col. iv. 14.

Jack. Oh, I am so sorry, I don't like doctors.

Mrs. H. I think you would have liked Luke though, Jack.

Ph. Why Mother, you say that just as if you had known him quite well!

Mrs. H. I do feel rather as if I had known him. It always strikes me there is so much character in the way he writes. Each of the Evangelists has his own way of telling the Story of Christ's life, and Luke writes his Gospel in such a natural, story-telling way, mentioning little things that happened, and that the other Evangelists (except Mark) would have been too much occupied with Jewish or Heavenly things to think of noticing.

Ph. Who was Theophilus, Mother?

Mrs. H. I don't know, except that he was a friend of Luke's. And that again makes his Gospel more homely and life-like, written as it is in the form of a letter, in order that his friend might have a true idea of the things that really happened. Luke seems not to have known the Lord Jesus Christ Himself when He was on earth—at any rate he never says he did. He begins with an account of John the Baptist, who was a man sent from God to prepare the way for His Son, by preaching repentance to Israel, and announcing the Coming of Jesus. That was such very important work that he was to be trained from the very first, and divinely fitted for it. His birth was peculiar, and so was his life, indeed everything about him was peculiar: he was quite a singular man. I mean that he was unlike anybody else. There had, however, been some whom God had raised up to do a great work in Old Testament times, who had been like him in some respects. Such as Isaac, and Samson, and Elijah. We shall see this presently, but now let us read our chapter, or at least part of it."

ZACHARIAS AND ELIZABETH.

Mrs. Hillyard then read Luke i. 1-23, explaining a word sometimes, to make it quite plain for the little ones. Then she said—
"This story is so clearly and simply told, I think you must all have understood it *if you listened*. Now, Elsie, suppose you try and tell *me* the story, that I may see how much you remember of it."

Elsie. Oh, I am sure I can tell you all about it, I liked the story so much—Once upon a time——

Myles. Stop a bit, Elsie—it isn't a fairy story, and "once upon a time" means nothing at all, You must tell us *where* it happened, and *when*, please.

E. Oh dear! I forget that—Myles, you say—

M. It happened in Judea, the little country in Asia now called Palestine. I'll show it you in the map presently, and the sketches Uncle Dick took there last year, too, if you like. And as for *when*, it was about 1880 years ago, and in the reign of "Herod the king"—that's enough for you now.

E. Well then,—once upon a time—I mean in the reign of Herod the king—there was a very good man called Zacharias, and he had a very good wife, and she——

J. I don't remember about their being so very good. God had to punish Zacharias for not believing His message.

E. But I *know* it said they were good, didn't it, Mother?

Mrs. H. Yes, Elsie, you are quite right, we are told "they were both righteous before God, walking in all the commandments and ordinances of the Lord, blameless." But that doesn't mean, as we find soon enough, that they never did wrong. Go on.

E. Well, his wife was called Elizabeth, and *wasn't* it funny her having the same name as me! I can always remember her by that. And Zacharias was a priest—Mother, what is a priest?

J. Oh Elsie! why, of course, a priest is a sort of a clergyman.

Mrs. H. Don't be in such a hurry, Jack; there was a great difference between a priest and a clergyman, though they are alike in being God's ministers* which means servants.

---

* Joel ii. 17; 1 Cor. iv. 1.

ZACHARIAS AND ELIZABETH.

The priests of the Old Testament were men of a certain family—the family of Aaron, Moses' brother—who were consecrated—that is set apart—for God's special service. Every man of that family was obliged to be a priest. There you see they were quite unlike clergymen. And their work was different too. What was their particular work, Phyllis?

Ph. To offer sacrifices.

Mrs. H. Yes, to offer sacrifices and to burn incense was their principal work. You know we left off reading Exodus when we got as far as the 21st chapter. I did not wish you to go on, because it was impossible the little ones could have understood all about the laws and ceremonies which God commanded the Israelites to keep and perform. Some day, Elsie, when you and Jack know a great deal more about the Lord Jesus Christ, and about what we, as Christians, are and ought to be, I hope you will go back and read the whole of the Old Testament carefully; and then you will understand something of what God meant by all the strange work the priests had to do. In the meantime you need not trouble your heads about them at all, for there are no such people now: there is not a priest like Zacharias remaining upon earth.* You can go on again now.

E. And so Zacharias was burning incense in the Temple, and the people were praying outside; and incense was stuff that smelt very nice when it was burning—sort of scented smoke like pastilles—and he burnt it because God had told the priests to burn it twice every day on a pretty gold table in the Temple. I forget what you said about the Temple, Mother.

Mrs. H. I said the Temple was the building outside which the sacrifices were killed and burnt on the altar; and where the people went to worship. It was called God's House. I will tell you more about it another time.

E. And whilst Zacharias was burning incense an angel came to him, and Zacharias was very frightened. But the angel told him not to be frightened, because his prayer was

---

* It would be out of place in this connection to enter upon such a subject as the "royal priesthood" of all believers who "offer up spiritual sacrifices," or upon that of the Christian Ministry.

heard, and Elizabeth was to have a son. Had he been praying for a son, Mother?

Mrs. H. Yes, no doubt he had, and yet he was so surprised when the answer came, that he wouldn't believe it.*

J. Mother, what was the angel like that came to Zacharias? Had it got great white wings?

Mrs. H. No, the same angel—Gabriel—is described by the prophet Daniel, to whom the Lord also sent him with a message, more than 500 years before, as being like a man, indeed, he calls him "the man Gabriel."† Whenever the Bible tells us about angels appearing to people, it always says they looked like men; and two or three times they are called "men," and not angels, which only means *messengers*. What is a messenger, Jack?

J. Some one that is sent with a message. But angels always have wings in pictures.

Mrs. H. Yes, dear, and we all feel the beauty and fitness of their being so represented, because it is meant to show us their readiness at all

---

* See also Acts xii. 15.   † Dan. ix. 21.

times to go quickly on God's errands. But real live angels haven't got wings all over feathers, of course, however beautiful they look in pictures.

M. I should hope not, they would be monsters if they had!

J. But if they haven't got wings how do they go up and down from earth to heaven?

Mrs. H. I don't know any more than you do, Jack. Indeed I know next to nothing about angels. There is so little said about them in the Bible.

J. But I do want to know more about them, because, you know, when we go to heaven we shall be angels ourselves.

M. I'm sure we *don't* know any such thing! Who ever told you that, Jack?

J. Ninny. She said little Mary was gone to be an angel in heaven; and she gave me a hymn to learn about

"I want to be an angel,
And with the angels stand."*

---

* A friend remarks that either Jack or Ninny had been guilty of a misquotation. The hymn probably intended runs:—
"I would be like an angel," &c.

Mrs. H. Well, dear child, you will never be an angel, I assure you, though I hope you will be a "messenger" for God, and do a great deal of work for Him. But Gabriel, and the angels we have read about, are a different class of people altogether from ourselves. They may be men—I think they are—but they have never been sinners, nor will they ever be amongst the number of those who have been "bought with the precious Blood of Christ." So you nèed not "want to be an angel," Jack, for if you really trust yourself to Jesus, you will be something better and higher than that, and nearer to Himself.

J. I shall be higher than Gabriel, Mother! You don't mean that, really?

Mrs. H. I do mean it most truly, though I know how very wonderful it is that we should have such a place: so wonderful, that we cannot the least realise it at present; but we may safely believe it and rejoice in it for all that, for this is what God has promised to them that love Him.* But poor Elsie is waiting all

---

* Compare Luke i. 19, with xii. 37, Eph. ii. 6, and Rev. iii. 21.

this time to finish her story. Go on, little one, we are all listening. You left off where Gabriel told Zacharias his prayer was heard, and he was to have a son.

E. Oh yes!—and the angel said they were to call the baby "John," and that they would all be so happy; and that John would be a great man, and would never drink wine or beer. But Zacharias didn't believe it all, and asked how he should know it was true, and then Gabriel said he should be dumb, and not able to say a word till John was born. And all this time while Zacharias and the angel were talking, the people were waiting and waiting, and wondering whatever had happened to him, and at last, when he did come, he couldn't speak, he could only make signs to them that something had happened; so they guessed he had seen something wonderful. After that he went on with his work in the Temple, till his time was up, and then he went home to his house. That's all I remember, is there anything more, Mumsey?

Mrs. H. Very little more, darling. You have told it very nicely. But there are just one or two things I want to remind you of. Remember it was said of John that he was to be "great *in the sight of the Lord*"—that is to say, he was not to be the sort of man that *people* generally admire, and call "Great:" nor would he be "great" in his own eyes, but *God* would think him "great," and call him so, too;* and he was to be from his very birth "filled with the Holy Ghost." You hardly know what that means now, but try to remember the *words* all the same. And another thing I want you to remember is this—that it is always the best plan to believe God at once, and act on what He says, without wanting a "sign," as poor Zacharias did. Not only does such want of confidence dishonour God, but the "sign," if it comes, is generally a *judgment*. Zacharias' "sign" did him no good. If he had only believed the message, and waited, he would have had quite "sign" enough when his son was born; he was no better off for being dumb first for nearly a year. And so if *we* only take God at His Word, we shall have plenty of "signs *following*," that will be much

---

* Luke vii. 28.

better for us than signs *beforehand*, and then we shall be spared many a judgment.

And now, as we are beginning Luke's Gospel, we will end our reading this morning with a short prayer, and use the words of the Collect for St. Luke's day in the Prayer Book.

Almighty God, Who calledst Luke the Physician, whose praise is in the Gospel, to be an Evangelist, and Physician of the Soul; May it please Thee that by the wholesome medicines of the doctrine delivered by him, all the diseases of our souls may be healed; through the merits of Thy Son Jesus Christ our Lord. Amen.

LORD JESUS, are we one with Thee?
  O height! O depth of Love!
With Thee we died upon the Tree,
  In Thee we live above.

Such was Thy Grace, that for our sake
  Thou didst from heaven come down;
Thou didst of flesh and blood partake,
  In all our sorrows one.

Our sins, our guilt, in Love Divine,
  Confessed and borne by Thee;
The gall, the curse, the wrath were Thine,
  To set Thy Members free.

Ascended now in glory bright,
  Still one with us Thou art ;
Nor life, nor death, nor depth, nor height,
  Thy saints and Thee can part.

Oh ! teach us, Lord, to know and own
  This wondrous mystery,
That Thou with us art truly one
  And we are one with Thee !

Soon, soon shall come that glorious Day,
  When, seated on Thy Throne,
Thou shalt to wondering worlds display
  That Thou with us art ONE !

JAMES G. DECK.

CHAPTER V.

MARY.

LUKE I. 26-79.

NEXT morning when they were all assembled under the mulberry tree on the lawn for their Bible lesson, Mrs. Hillyard said, "You will hear more about the angel Gabriel to-day. He was sent by God this time with a more wonderful message than he can ever have given to any one before. But I will *tell* the story to Jack and Elsie to-day, as nearly in the words of the Bible as I can, for them to understand it.

"About six months after the visit of Gabriel to Zacharias in the Temple, God sent him to a city, or rather what we should call a village of Galilee, named Nazareth; to a young girl called Mary, a cousin of Elizabeth's, who was engaged to be married to a man named Joseph, of the 'house,' that is, family of David. That was the Royal Family, for David was King of Israel about a thousand years before, and Joseph's ancestors had been kings of Israel or of Judah as long as the Jews had a king of their own, and that was until they were carried away captive to Babylon.

"But though Joseph was of the royal family, he was a poor man, and was thought nothing of even in Nazareth, and Nazareth was a place very much despised by the Jews. He was only a poor carpenter, and had to work hard for his bread."

Jack. But how ever did he come down so low as that, if he was of the Royal family? Surely none of our Queen's great-grandchildren would ever be common carpenters?

Mrs. Hillyard. Well, perhaps not; though even in England some of the members of the oldest families have known strange reverses of fortune. But the history of the Jews was very different from the history of England. Our country has had its ups and downs as all countries have had, but still for more than a thousand years it has been making steady progress in civilisation, and commerce, and wealth; but Judea had never been out of trouble hardly. The Jews, though we call them "God's favoured people," had had about as stormy a history as any people could have. They had always been surrounded by enemies much stronger than themselves, who were continually fighting with them. About three hundred years after David died, that is to say, about seven hundred years before Luke's Gospel begins, the Assyrians had carried off ten out of the twelve tribes of Israel as prisoners to their own land; and nobody knows what has become of them, they have never been heard of since. Then about a hundred years after that, nearly all the remaining Israelites—the tribes of Judah and Benjamin—were carried away by the King of Babylon and remained his servants for seventy years. They came back again to their own land, and after that were called Jews, and they rebuilt the wall round Jerusalem, and the Temple, which had been destroyed, but they never enjoyed any prosperity, or even peace, for more than two or three years together.

Their history up to the Christian era (that is to

say, till the birth of Christ) was a succession of struggles with various enemies. They never had a real king of their own again, but were governed, when any government was possible, by their high priests; whilst Judea was tributary to the Persians, the Egyptians, the Grecians, and the Romans successively. So you can fancy that in such stormy times as those, all the old families got a thorough upset; and the land had been so impoverished, and the Jews had to pay such heavy tribute to their conquerors, that nearly all of them must have been very poor.

Joseph and Mary had been neighbours, as both lived at Nazareth. We are not told anything in the Bible about Mary's parents, so very likely they were both dead. Neither is it mentioned with whom she was living when the angel came to her—perhaps with her married sister, as we know she had one.

"And the angel came in unto her, and said, Hail, thou that art highly favoured, the Lord is with thee: blessed art thou' among women. And when she saw him, she was troubled at his saying, and cast in her mind what manner of salutation this should be." What does "salutation" mean, Phyllis?

Phyllis. Does it mean *greeting?*

Mrs. H. Yes. But it was not the sort of greeting that a poor girl like Mary was accustomed to receive, so no wonder she was surprised! "And the angel said unto her, Fear not, Mary: for thou hast found favour with God. And behold thou shalt bring forth a Son, and shalt call His name JESUS. He shall be great, and shall be called the Son of the Highest: and the Lord God shall give unto Him the Throne of His father David: and He shall reign over the house of Jacob for ever; and of His Kingdom there shall be no end."

Mary did not behave like Zacharias, for though she wondered very much at the angel's message, and asked him how it should happen, she doesn't seem to have doubted for a moment that God would do as He said. And then the angel went on to explain to her that her Son should be the Son of God; and he told her too that her cousin Elizabeth would also soon have a child; and that, however strange these things might be, "with God nothing shall be impossible." And Mary said, "Behold the handmaid of the Lord; be it unto me according to thy word."

When the angel Gabriel had left her, she went a journey into the hill country with haste, to a city of Judah, a great many miles off, to the house of Zacharias, to see her cousin Elizabeth, and congratulate her on the prospect of having a son, and to tell her too, I suppose, about the wonderful promise that had been made to *her*. But Elizabeth knew all about it before she could tell her, and being "filled with the Holy Ghost," she began at once to bless Mary, and to say what an honour she felt it that the mother of her Lord should come to her. The words of the blessing with which she blessed Mary are these, and it was God's own blessing—" Blessed is she which believed that there shall be a performance of those things which were told her from the Lord."* Such sweet, simple faith in God, as Mary showed, was sure to have His Blessing on it. And though it has pleased the Lord in His Wisdom to tell us so little about her, and nothing at all of her earlier life, still we may be quite sure that

* Margin.

this was not the first time she had trusted Him and believed what He said. She must have long known and loved Him, most likely ever since she was a little child, to be so sure at once that it was His Voice* that spoke to her through His messenger. Though she was quite a young girl—most likely hardly older than Phyllis, for girls marry so very young in the East—yet, you see, she knew God better than Zacharias did, though he was a priest, and grown quite an old man in His service. Phyllis, I hope you can say by heart the beautiful song of praise she said.

Phyllis then repeated—"My soul doth magnify the Lord, and my spirit hath rejoiced in God my Saviour. For He hath regarded the low estate of His handmaiden: for, behold, from henceforth all generations shall call me blessed. For He that is mighty hath done to me great things ; and holy is His Name. And His mercy is on them that fear Him from generation to generation. He hath showed strength with His arm ; He hath scattered the proud in the imagination of their hearts, He hath put

---
* John x. 4, 5, as contrasted with 1 Kings xiii. 18, 19.

down the mighty from their seats, and exalted them of low degree. He hath filled the hungry with good things, and the rich He hath sent empty away. He hath holpen His servant Israel, in remembrance of His mercy; as He spake to our fathers, to Abraham, and to his seed for ever."

Mrs. H. Thank you, dear. How beautiful it is! One doesn't know which to admire most, Mary's rejoicing faith, or her deep humility. God had indeed fitted her by His grace to be the mother of Him Who was "meek and lowly of heart." She was so truly humble. We see nothing in her of that sort of humility—if we can call it so—that puts itself forward. She does not even talk about not being worthy. Worthy! of course, she was not worthy! How could any poor sinner be worthy of such an honour as God was about to put upon her? Her *un*worthiness was a matter of course, and in her great joy she lost sight of it altogether, and "rejoiced in *God her Saviour.*" She was just the very one for Him to choose for such a high calling, and for Jesus to come and live with.*

---

* Isaiah lvii. 15; John xiv. 23.

And what an insight she showed, too, into God's Word. She knew at once that His promise to her was the same that He had made to her forefather Abraham so long before. She had been expecting the " Man from the Lord "* as poor Eve had been—the Messiah of Israel—and she knew that her Son would be He. Elsie, have you been able to understand what we have been talking about?

Elsie. Yes, Mumsey, pretty well — but I want to know why Mary was called the "Virgin."

Mrs. H. I am glad you asked, darling: "Virgin" only means a girl who is not married. It is an old-fashioned word, and is hardly ever used now except in speaking of our Lord's Mother. We call her the "Virgin" because I suppose we generally think of her as she was when we first hear of her. She was a Virgin when Jesus was born, but she married Joseph afterwards. We often call her "blessed" too, as she said, "all generations" should; and well we may, for she was doubly blest. She had a

---

* Gen. iv. 1.

greater blessing than even being the Mother of Jesus; what was that, Phyllis?

Ph. Greater! I can't think of anything greater.

Mrs. H. Don't you remember that once when Jesus was preaching and a woman called out something about how "blessed" His Mother was, Jesus answered her—"Yea, rather, blessed are they that hear the Word of God and keep it"? I think He meant, that though of course it was a wonderfully "blessed" thing to be His Mother, and so closely related to Him in the flesh—yet the *greater* blessing was to know Him spiritually, and to do His will.* I have no doubt that when Jesus said that, He was thinking of the wonderful faith and humility with which Mary received God's words, and treasured them up in her heart.

Ph. But that is a blessing anybody may have.

Mrs. H. Just so, that is the beauty of it! We may all share Mary's greatest blessing, if we will. But we must go on with our

---

* See also Matt. xii. 46-50.

F

chapter and see what happened in Zacharias' family.

E. Oh yes! I do so want to hear about the baby John.

Mrs. H. I will read the rest of the story, for I know I couldn't tell it as plainly as St. Luke does; you will all understand this part.

Mrs. Hillyard then read verses 57 to 66.

She then said, "Now, Myles, it is your turn to say something by heart, so please repeat Zacharias' song which I am sure you know, you hear it so often in church."

Myles. All right, Mother, but I do want to say just one thing first. Wasn't Zacharias deaf as well as dumb, as they had to make signs to him?

Mrs. H. Yes, I suppose he must have been, by that.

Myles then repeated verses 68 to 79, and afterwards he said, " Zacharias seems at last to have understood it all as well as Mary did—doesn't he, Mother?"

Mrs. H. Through a special revelation to him he did. But you see it is said of him, as it is of his wife, that he was "filled with the Holy Ghost," and also that he "prophesied." We are not told that of Mary. Perhaps she did not need such extraordinary teaching, and *her* song rushed to her lips from the fulness of a heart in abiding fellowship with God, and running over with praise. Jack, can you tell me who Zacharias meant by "thou child" in the 76th verse?

J. Why, his own child John, Mother, of course.

Mrs. H. Quite right, and now which of you can tell me who is meant by the "Dayspring" in the 78th verse?

Ph. The "Dayspring"? I didn't know it meant any person at all.

Mrs. H. And don't you know either, Myles?

M. Well, I see now that it must mean Christ, but I never thought of it before. I wonder what I did think it meant, when I sang it in Church! Isn't it stupid the way words that one knows very well, run in one's head without one's *thinking* about them at all?

Mrs. H. Yes—so that if we don't mind, our very familiarity with the words seems to rob them of their sense. I have found that myself very often. But now, Myles, look in your Bible, —it is a Bagster, isn't it?—and between the Old and New Testaments, amongst other useful things, you will find a list of the "Titles of Christ," and amongst them you will, I think, see the "Dayspring"—as quoted from this passage.

M. Oh yes, here it is, there are a lot put together that are all about "Light," and this is one of them.

Mrs. H. And one of the most beautiful of all those beautiful Names. Yes, Jesus is the "Dayspring." The dawn was just breaking when John the Baptist was born; and then "Through the tender mercy of our God" the "Light of the world," the "Sun of Righteousness arose." He came, as I told you before, that men might see God—"To give light to them that sit in darkness. . . . And to guide our feet into the way of peace."—"The darkness is past and the True Light now shineth."

Lord Jesus, our Brother, and our Saviour, we cannot see Thee with our eyes, nor hear Thy Voice, nor ever minister unto Thine own Bodily necessities; but we thank Thee that, by Thy Goodness, we may yet share the

THE SUN-RISING.

greater blessing granted to Thy beloved Mother—that of keeping Thy word in our hearts, and doing the will of our Father in Heaven. Grant to us the fulness of this Blessing for Thine own Sake. Amen.

WE needs must love that Mother dear
   Whom Jesus loves so well,
And to His Glory, year by year,
   Her praise and honour tell.

Bound with the curse of sin and shame
   We helpless sinners lay,
Until in tender love He came
   To bear the curse away.

And her He chose from whom to take
   His own Humanity ;
In it to suffer for our sake,
   In it to make us free.

Her Babe He lay upon her breast,
   To her He cried for food ;
Her gentle nursing soothed to rest
   Th' Incarnate Son of God.

O wondrous depth of Grace Divine,
   That He should bend so low !
And, Mary, oh ! what joy 'twas thine
   In His dear love to know ;

Joy to be Mother of the Lord,
   But bliss yet deeper still,

Meekly to hear His Holy Word
And do His Blessed Will !

Jesus, the Virgin's Holy Son,
 We praise Thee and adore,
Who art with God the Father One
 And Spirit evermore.

Adapted from
Hymns Ancient and Modern.

CHAPTER VI.
GOOD NEWS.

LUKE ii. 1-20.

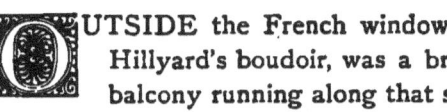UTSIDE the French windows of Mrs. Hillyard's boudoir, was a broad stone balcony running along that side of the house, not very high above the ground, and from which a flight of steps led down to the flower garden. It was a favourite seat of hers in the summer time, for the awning overhead kept off the sun, whilst the balustrade on either side was wreathed with creepers.

Here Mrs. Hillyard and her four children met for their next Bible reading, and a picturesque little group they were, seated in their light summer dresses on deep red cushions, whilst upon the steps reposed in various attitudes three dogs—one of them an enormous drab-coloured English mastiff—and a tortoiseshell cat with two kittens; all the best of friends, unless some exceptional circumstance, such as a dog appropriating another's bone, or the puppy of the party playing a little too roughly with one of the kittens, created a temporary disturbance. They were all far too sleepy, however, for any diversion of that kind just now, and there appeared no danger of their distracting the children's attention; so Mrs. Hillyard told Jack to hand round the Bibles.

Mrs. Hillyard. There may be some things in our chapter to-day which you will not understand very well, but a great deal I know you will find quite plain if you pay attention. I will tell you all the first part as I did yesterday, because some verses require a little explaining; but I shall use the words of the Bible wherever I can.

Elsie. Mother, when *are* we coming to Jesus Himself?

Mrs. H. Bless you, my darling, for wanting to come to Him! This morning we shall really read about Him, though only as a little Baby. I will begin now—"And it came to pass in those days, that there went out a decree from Cæsar Augustus, that all the world should be taxed." Myles, you know, of course, who Augustus Cæsar was?

Myles. Yes, the Emperor of Rome.

Mrs. H. And this "taxing" was what is now called a *census*. What is that, Phyllis?

Phyllis. Why, it is the government sending round to take down everybody's name, and age, and trade, and all sorts of things;—I remember quite well the man coming here, when we were little; don't you, Myles? But I haven't a notion what it was all for.

Mrs. H. The principal object of a census is to find out how many people there are in the country. It may also be necessary to ascertain other facts about them, but in the case of this old Roman census, I suppose just to count the people was the chief thing. The Emperor wanted to know how many subjects he had, and so gave orders that all his dominions should be "taxed," or "enrolled," as you see it is in the margin of our Bibles.

Ph. But why does Luke say that "all the world should be taxed"?

Mrs. H. The Roman empire was commonly called "the world," and indeed it did contain all the civilised world then. The people in it hardly knew anything about the rest of mankind, whom they used to speak of as "the barbarians." Judea was then tributary to the Romans, and subject to them, and so was considered as part of the empire, but still it had nominally a king of its own at that time, and was not yet a Roman province.* Perhaps it may have been not to offend the Jews more than he could help, that the Roman governor ordered the enrolment to be made in the Jewish fashion instead of the Roman. The Romans always counted the people as we do now, putting down their names at the places where they were living; but the Jews, who were so careful with regard to their genealogies, used to go to the town to which their family first belonged, and were enrolled there. Now David's own particular town was Bethlehem,† so there Joseph went as his descendant; and Mary went with him, because she too was of the family of David, and

---

* Gen. xlix. 10. † 1 Sam. xvii. 12.

GOOD NEWS. 91

of an * older branch of it, most likely, than the kingly line to which Joseph † belonged. St. Matthew tells us that before they started, the angel of the Lord appeared to Joseph in a dream, and told him that Mary was soon to have a Son Whose Father was God Himself, and that he was to "call His Name JESUS, for He shall save His people from their sins." And the angel also said that this would be a fulfilment of that which the Lord had spoken by Isaiah the prophet,‡ saying, that a virgin should have a Son, and that His Name should be called "Emmanuel," which means "God with us." Mary's going to Bethlehem all alone with Joseph, looks again as if she had no parents, or brothers, or near kinsmen belonging to her at Nazareth. It was a long journey, and very likely they had to walk most part of

---

* Luke iii. 31 ; 2 Sam. v. 14.
† Matt. 1. 6. The genealogy in Luke iii., being probably that of Mary, who is mentioned by a Rabbinical writer in the Talmud as being the daughter of Heli. See Lightfoot's "Hebrew and Talmudical Exercitations on St. Luke." In that case Joseph would be identified with Mary on the principle laid down in Num. xxxvi. 8 : the "inheritance" in the case of the B. V. lying in abeyance.
‡ Isa. vii. 14.

the way, being quite poor people; and no doubt Mary was very tired when they got there.

"And so it was, that while they were there . . . she brought forth her first-born Son, and wrapped Him in swaddling clothes, and laid Him in a manger; because there was no room for them in the inn." In these few and simple words St. Luke tells the wonderful Story of the Coming into this world of the Son of God—and it is all that God ever tells us about it. The world went on as if nothing particular had happened, and the people in the little town of Bethlehem, which was just then all in a bustle with the strangers coming in, and filling every corner of it, probably never gave a thought to the poor carpenter and his wife who had arrived too late to get any room in the inn. And yet the birth of this little baby in the cattle shed* was the grand event to which the Old Testament with all its types and prophecies was ever pointing. And this was the most wonderful Day that had ever dawned in the whole world's history— the Day that Abraham had rejoiced to behold by

---

* Probably a cave or grotto, still often used as a shelter for camels and mules, in connection with an Eastern Khan.

THE SHEPHERDS AT BETHLEHEM.

faith nearly 2000 years before, and which the prophets and kings had desired to see in vain.

Jack. But, Mother, nobody could know that that baby was God's Son if He never told them so. Why didn't He tell everybody? He might have sent down all the angels in heaven, to blow their trumpets, and say Christ was coming.

E. And then why didn't He come some grander way?

Ph. It does seem odd, doesn't it, Mother, that He should choose to come just that way?

Mrs. H. It does seem very strange, if we judge God's ways according to our notions of what would have been fitting. The only answer to the questions you have been asking is simply— God did not choose to come into the world at that time in any other than the way He did come; therefore, that was the best way, and the only way. "The Kingdom of God" certainly did not come then "with observation," that is with pomp or show, and I think we may venture to say that it did not, for one chief reason, because the only way into that Kingdom was to be by *faith*, and there could have been no such thing as faith, if God had forced people to believe in His Son. And we must remember, too, that Jesus came to make people good,* and it would have made no one any better to have known that He was in the world—why should it? The hearts of sinners had to be purified by† faith before the presence of God could be any blessing to them. I will explain to Elsie what "faith" means another time, but now we must go on, and you will see that God really did do something like what Jack said—He did send down His angels in great glory to say Christ had come. But He did not send the message to the world, only to a few shepherds, who, I suppose, were already "waiting" for Him, like some other people we shall read about presently.

J. Oh yes, I know all the story of the shepherds quite well.

E. And so do I, Mumsey, only it seems so funny to be reading it in the hot weather out of doors, instead of at Christmas time. It is a Christmas story, isn't it, Jack?

J. Yes, but it will do any time. Did it really happen at Christmas time, Mother? It must

---

* Matt. i. 21.   † Acts xv. 9.

have been awfully cold for the shepherds, being out all night in the fields, in the snow.

Mrs. H. For one thing you know, Jack, it is much warmer in Palestine than it is here; and for another, it probably did not happen in the winter at all. It is much more likely to have been either in the spring-time—about April,* or in September;† in either case it would then have been quite warm weather there. Most Christians have always liked to keep the Lord's birthday, and so for many centuries they have done so on the 25th of December, but they couldn't keep the real day, for they didn't know it. Good Friday and Easter Sunday are quite different, for they are generally the real days, according to the Jewish reckoning, on which Christ died and rose again.

Ph. Why did people fix on the 25th of December, to keep Christ's birthday?

Mrs. H. When Christmas was first kept by the early Christians, there can hardly be any doubt that they chose that time, because it was just about then that two great heathen festivals

---

* See Dr. Alford on this passage in "New Testament for English Readers." † Lightfoot's Works, iii. 25, 40.

were celebrated—the Saturnalia, and the Brumalia. Probably, they thought they could gain over the heathens round them, by keeping a festival at the same time they did; only keeping it in honour of Christ, whilst the rest were commemorating Saturn or Mithras.

Ph. But that was very wrong, wasn't it?

Mrs. H. It seems very shocking to us; but we should be careful how we pronounce judgment on people living in days so different from ours, and of whom we know so little, certainly.

M. But the Saturnalia was a perfect proverb of wickedness. It does seem awful to mix up a Christian festival with it.

Mrs. H. Yes, it does. You see there was a time when the persecution of Christians began to cease, and heathenish customs got mixed up with their religious observances. Then those who were Christians merely in name got the upper hand, and they would naturally turn even the Birth of Christ into a pretext for riot and pleasuring. But really there is so much of the same spirit in the Christmas pleasuring of what we call " Christian England " at the present day, that I think we ought to take that more to heart, before we are very severe on the ignorant Christians of those barbarous days.

M. Well, it is not a pleasant idea, that our Christmas is merely an adaptation of a heathen festival! Is it, Mother?

Mrs. H. No, it is not. But there is another way of looking at it. The Roman Brumalia was borrowed from the Mythology of the Persians, who worshipped the sun under the name of Mithras, and at the time of the winter solstice, when the days were beginning to lengthen again, they kept the birthday of the sun, which may be said at that time to be born anew. Then as Christianity grew and strengthened, it is very probable that an attempt was made to consecrate this festival by keeping it in honour of the Birth of the Sun of Righteousness. This is certainly a beautiful idea, and one which almost reconciles us to what may have been too time-serving a policy on the part of the early Christians.

M. Yes. I hope that was it.

Mrs. H. I think there is very little doubt that it was so. The Emperor Constantine combined the two ideas in the inscription round some

G

of the coins of his day. Like all human institutions, the keeping of days is a mixture of good and evil. Indeed even the observing of Sunday has been terribly abused. But those are no reasons why such commemorations should not be a blessing to us.* It depends on ourselves, I think, whether they are or not. They are a great spiritual help and comfort to many people.

J. It is not wrong to have fun at Christmas time, is it?

Mrs. H. Not wrong at all, I think, dear. When we are celebrating the time that Jesus came to tell people how good and kind His Father was, and how He would like everybody and everything to be happy, it can hardly be wrong for us to enjoy ourselves, especially if we are young and merry; so long, of course, as our amusements are not sinful.

Mrs. Hillyard then read Luke ii. 8–20, whilst the children followed her in their Bibles. Afterwards she said—

"This beautiful story is told with such Divine

---

* Rom. xiv. 5, 6, 13.

simplicity, that we feel that if any more had been added to it, it would have been less grand. It is just perfect as it is, every word of it. And so, as I know you all understand it—as well as any one needs to do—I think we won't talk about it, please, for we should only spoil it. But let us try by God's grace to keep these things in our hearts, as the Blessed Virgin did, and think them over alone. Our lesson has been short to-day, but it is a very important one; and we may go away as the shepherds did, praising and blessing God for the 'good tidings of great joy' that He has made known to us. For the Gospel is ours just as much as theirs, and the word Gospel, as you all know, means 'Good News,' and it *is* Good News, every word of it, from first to last."

Mrs. Hillyard's prayer that morning was in these words—

Almighty God, Who hast given us Thy only-begotten Son to take our nature upon Him, and to be born of a pure Virgin; Grant that we being born again, and made Thy children by adoption and grace, may daily be renewed by Thy Holy Spirit; through the same, our

THE HOLY CHILDHOOD.

Lord Jesus Christ, Who liveth and reigneth with Thee and the same Spirit, ever One God, world without end. Amen.
(*Collect for Christmas Day.*)

I LOVE to hear the story
  Which Angel voices tell,
How once the King of Glory
  Came down on earth to dwell.
I am both weak and sinful,
  But this I surely know,
The Lord came down to save me,
  Because He loved me so.
    I love to hear the story
      Which Angel voices tell,
    How once the King of Glory
      Came down on earth to dwell.

I'm glad my Blessed Saviour
  Was once a Child like me,
To show how pure and holy
  His little ones might be;
He'll teach me how to follow
  His footsteps here below,
And never will forget me,
  Because He loves me so.
    I love to hear the story
      Which Angel voices tell,
    How once the King of Glory
      Came down on earth to dwell.

To sing His love and mercy
  My sweetest song I'll raise,
And though I cannot see Him
  I know He hears my praise;
For He has kindly promised
  That even I may go
To sing among His Angels,
  Because He loves me so.
    I love to hear the story
      Which Angel voices tell,
    How once the King of Glory
      Came down on earth to dwell.
                    E. H. MILLER.

CHAPTER VII.

CIRCUMCISION.

LUKE II. 21.

HE whole time of the Bible reading next morning was taken up by a conversation on Luke ii. 21.

Mrs. Hillyard. We must always remember that as a Man, our Lord Jesus Christ was a Jew. Indeed the Evangelists will not allow us to forget this. In reading the Story of His Life on earth, we are reminded of it at every point— from His Birth at the city of His ancestor David, to His dying words upon the Cross, "It is finished," referring, as He did even then, to the last and complete fulfilment of the Jewish ceremonial law. Now I have used some hard words, but if the little ones listen to me, and notice *how* I use them, they will very soon

CIRCUMCISION. 103

understand what they mean. I wonder if Elsie can tell me what a "law" is.

Elsie. Doesn't it mean things that you must do, or else you'll be punished?

Mrs. H. Yes, a "law" means the words in which you were told by some one you are bound to obey, that you must, or must not do so and so. If I forbid you ever to poke the fire, that is a law. Or if I say, you must never sit down to dinner without having first washed your hands, that is a law. Now God has given many laws to different people—tell me one, Elsie.

E. He told Adam and Eve not to eat the fruit.

Jack. And He gave the Israelites the Ten Commandments.

Mrs. H. You are both quite right. He also gave a great many very strange laws or commandments to the Jews. They had to do many things that they didn't understand, just as children have to do now; and these orders from God to the people, through Moses, are called the "ceremonial laws," because they were laws about *ceremonies*. What does that mean, Jack?

J. I don't quite know, but isn't being married a ceremony? I know I have heard people say, "The ceremony was performed by Mr. So-and-so."

Mrs. H. Yes, little man, you are quite right. Certain performances that anybody can see, must be done at a marriage, for it to be a real marriage according to the law of the country. A funeral may be called a ceremony too. When the Queen was crowned, that was a ceremony. But none of these things are ordered by God directly. The only ceremonies, or rites (which is another word for the same thing), that God has ordered for us as Christians, are those two which people call "Sacraments"—Baptism, and the Lord's Supper. The Jews' ceremonies, and our Sacraments, are alike in this that they are both as it were *acted pictures* of Christ's Blessed Death and Resurrection; but there is this great difference, the Jews' ceremonies pictured that which had not yet happened, and therefore it was impossible for them clearly to understand what the picture, or type, meant. But our Sacraments are pictures of what *has* happened, and what we know all about, and therefore we ought to understand what they mean. Now you all know that the sacrifices of bullocks, and of lambs, and of goats, were pictures of the Death upon the Cross of our Blessed Saviour, and that *their* blood was *His* Blood in a figure. But the offering of animals on God's Altar was not nearly all the picture-teaching of the Jews' ceremonial law. Lots of other things were to be done, some of them seeming even to us, who can understand them so much better than the Jews could, very strange indeed—but all of them, whether we understand them or not, showing forth some part of the perfection of the Person or the Work of Christ. And when He came, He was obliged, as an Israelite, to obey all these laws, although they were being fulfilled in Himself; for they were not all fulfilled till He had died upon the Cross. Then the strange Picture-Book, by which the Jews had been led to look for their Redeemer, was torn up.* It had taught them, or ought to have taught them about Him, and so "was the schoolmaster to bring them to Christ." † But when all the types

---

* Matt. xxvii. 51. † Gal. iii. 24.

were fulfilled, this course of lessons was no longer needed, and God taught people in a different way.

J. Had God taught any other people besides the Jews in that sort of way?

Mrs. H. No, these object lessons, or teaching through symbols, had been only for Israel. The history of Job shows us that He had taught some Gentiles to offer sacrifices to Him, but that was all, as far as we know; unto Israel alone had been "committed the oracles of God." Therefore He had chosen them to very special honour;* and it was through the Seed, or Descendant of Abraham † (Christ), that " all the nations of the earth " were to be "blessed." ‡ The Jews were a "peculiar people," and were to consider themselves so, and to behave as such, and as a token of God's Covenant with Abraham, and as a sign of separation from the rest of the world, who were called " Gentiles," they were to be circumcised. This rite fenced them off, as it were, from other people, and marked them as God's chosen ones. It was

---

* Rom. iii. 2; ix. 4, 5; Deut. iv. 8; vii. 6.
† Gal. iii. 16.   ‡ Gen. xxii. 18.

very strictly enforced—that is, ordered on pain of punishment. You will find this in Genesis xvii. 10–14.

(Myles read the passage.)

Mrs. H. Circumcision is still practised by the Jews. It is a cutting and tearing away of part of the skin of the body, and is a very painful operation.

Phyllis. But, Mother, it seems so horrid and cruel to hurt a poor little baby like that! Surely, something else might have been done instead?

Mrs. H. If circumcision had been *only* to mark the Israelites as God's peculiar people, something else might have been done instead, I daresay: but there was something more in it than that. They were circumcised as the kinsmen of the Great Sufferer—the Crucified Saviour—the bleeding Lamb of God.

Here we enter upon a very deep and mysterious subject, which it is well perhaps that even children should face—the necessity of suffering. My darlings, even you know a little, already, of what pain is. You will know more and more what it means. The world is full of misery, and suffering, and death. It is very terrible, and the more we try to do a little good, and if possible to make the wretchedness round us a little less, the more are we bowed down with the hopelessness, almost, of our task, and with the awful reality of evil. Now what causes it?

Myles. Sin.

Mrs. H. And who is the active agent in it?

Ph. The devil.

Mrs. H. Yes, these words are soon said; God alone knows what they mean. But He has told us this much, that Sin and Suffering must go together. Now the world is full of sin—corrupted, poisoned by it; therefore we ought not to wonder that it is full of suffering, for what God has joined together cannot be put asunder.

M. Mother, haven't you ever wondered why God let the world get into such a state, and allowed the devil to have such power?

Mrs. H. Of course I have; who could help it? But God has given us no clue to that mystery. The immensity of the evil, and the strength of Satan's kingdom of darkness, can only be dimly guessed at, when we remember that even God could not save us without becoming a Sufferer—a Sufferer even unto Death! All we can do is just to accept the fact that God's Work, once "very good," is now very bad—bad at its very heart. But that to all who will have it, He offers a Remedy which will eventually destroy * evil, and will now give us still greater Good. And that is? . . . .

Ph. Jesus.

Mrs. H. Yes—so that by receiving Him, we are "delivered from the power of darkness, and translated" (or raised up into) "the kingdom of God's dear Son." For Jesus has sounded evil to its depths, and alone can triumph over it. Therefore it was fitting that He should commence His earthly Life by suffering — and He was circumcised.

M. Was circumcision a type of anything?

Mrs. H. It was typical too, no doubt: but I cannot explain to you, nor would you understand, all the deep teaching it was meant to convey, neither, therefore, why the outward rite was exactly what it was. As far as I understand and can explain the truth it was intended to

---

* Hub. ii. 14.

show forth, it is this—that a Christian ought to be, and in some measure is, a person who is denying himself, and taking up his cross, and following Jesus. I told you that the Gospel was all good news, and so it is; for without it we should be lost and miserable for ever, but the safety and happiness which it promises us come from our Master's Agony and Death. If we follow Him as disciples through this world of sin, it won't be all plain sailing for us. There will be plenty of trials, and difficulties, and temptations for us to meet with, but the most painful part of our fight, by far, will be with our own bad habits, and the desires of our own evil hearts. For though Christ's followers have a Joy that the world cannot give or take away, they have a struggle with "the sin* that dwelleth in them," of the bitterness of which the world knows nothing.

J. Still, taking it all together, I should hope Christians were happier than other people?

Mrs. H. Of course: God wants us to be happy, and has given Christ to make us so, but we can't ever be happy whilst we let

---

* Rom. vii. 20.

the evil in us get the upper hand. There is a Collect somewhere in the Prayer-Book, that speaks of "continually mortifying our corrupt affections." Have any of you an idea what that means?

M. I think I have, Mother, but I couldn't tell you.

Mrs. H. Then I will try and tell *you.* It means—continually putting to death, or making dead, our liking for what is bad. Phyllis, get that Alford's Testament from the table, and look for Colossians iii. 5. You will see that he renders the word "mortify" there as I did. And now, Myles, I ask you, because you know something of this "mortifying" process—*is it a pleasant one?*

Myles' "No" had a good deal of meaning in it.

Mrs. H. Some of this suffering every sinner has to go through that God takes into Covenant with Himself; but it is people's own fault that it is as bad as it is. It would not be nearly so bad if we didn't let our evil habits and desires get so strong. We should keep them under from the very first by the Power of that Grace

God is always ready to give us. Some people who have not done this, could tell you that they would rather have bits of their flesh pinched out with red-hot pincers, than have to tear an idol from their hearts. Indeed, when it comes to that, which it never should do, God does it for them, but even then it hurts terribly. Still the more we know of Him, the more thankful we feel that we have to do with One Who is possessed of what is perhaps the noblest form of courage, and never shrinks from giving pain to those He loves.

Ph. Mumsey, do you remember Father burning out that place on my chin where Puck bit me? I do so well, though I was so little. I knew he couldn't be cruel, but I remember thinking it so odd that he should hurt me so. And afterwards he began to cry.

Mrs. H. Yes, darling, I remember it quite well, and I am glad you do; but try and remember too, always, in spite of appearances, that our Father in Heaven has a still more tender Heart. He is obliged to hurt us sometimes, and to punish us, and the way He mostly does this is by letting us punish* ourselves, allowing us to reap as we have sown. If we *will* indulge in Sin, we must expect the consequence, and the consequence will be, I have not the smallest doubt, that the bad habits we have formed will be a continual trouble and pain to us.

Ph. So that the suffering, after all, comes more from ourselves than from God.

Mrs. H. No doubt, in one sense, though like all evil, it is working out God's purposes. And this suffering from the "flesh" (that means the evil in us) is so real, that horrid as circumcision was, it was not at all too horrid to represent the suffering sin brings. You know that in the "Baptismal Service" of the Church of England, the baby is signed with the sign of the Cross—the instrument of torture on which Jesus died as the Sin-Bearer. Very likely the people who invented that custom, had this same idea in their minds that is taught in Circumcision, only as making the sign of the

---

* As in Isa. lxiv. 7, "There is none that calleth upon Thy Name, that stirreth up himself to take hold of Thee: therefore Thou hast hid Thy face from us, and *hast delivered us up into the hand of our iniquities.*"—(Bishop Lowth's translation.)

H

Cross on a child's forehead doesn't hurt, it is not nearly so vivid a picture as that which God gave in the Jews' Picture-Book of Types. Whenever He had to illustrate sin, it was always by something horrid.

J. Like the leprosy you were telling us about the other day, Mother.

Mrs. H. I was just going to say so. Nothing could be more loathsome than that disease, and it is one of the chief types of sin in the Old Testament. And though the Lord's "tender mercies are over all His works," and He would not unnecessarily hurt even a little bird in its nest;* yet when He had to draw a picture of the Sin-Bearer, He was obliged for truth's sake to do so by the sacrifice of poor innocent little lambs. People sometimes try to explain away these things, and to make out they were not so very revolting after all; but exactly in proportion as they do so, they weaken the force of the type. God was determined to show sin in its true colours, and judgment too, even though the streets of Jeru-

---

* Deut. xxii. 6, 7.

salem ran with blood.* It was worth while, and necessary, or He would not have done it.

Ph. I am so glad you have told us all that, I never could bear to think of all those horrible sacrifices.

Mrs. H. But, dear Phyllis, if it was so dreadful to think of the death of goats and lambs—and animals, after all, are killed in very much larger numbers in our own butchers' shops—how should we feel when we think of That which was the fulfilment of these types?"

There was a long pause after that, and then Mrs. Hillyard continued—

"But although circumcision was a typical rite, you must remember that it did not in any way set forth the Atoning Work of Christ; it was the child's own blood that was shed, not that of a substitute. And it was *only* a typical rite. It had no influence on the character. It never made any one holy. The Jews were as *un*holy a people in character as any on earth: and they were never allowed to suppose that they were any the better for

---

* 1 Kings viii. 63; 2 Chron. xxxv. 7, &c.

being circumcised, or that God would favour them on that account. Over and over again He told them this, as for instance in Jeremiah ix. 25, 26, which I should like you to read, please, Phyllis, and then Jack may read Romans ii. 28, 29."

After these passages had been read Myles inquired,

"Mother, why were only the men circumcised?"

Mrs. H. Well, the women were represented by the men, and were supposed to be circumcised in them, just as we are said to have died, when Christ our Head died. You will find 1 Cor. xi. 3, throw light on that point, I think. And so, because Jesus was an Israelite, and therefore bound to fulfil the law, He was circumcised, and not because He had any evil tendencies in His own spotless Nature. The blood which He then shed was not Atoning Blood—He never bore our sins until He hung upon the Cross*—but it consecrated for Him the path of Suffering which He had to tread,

---

* 1 Peter iii. 18.

CIRCUMCISION.

and which ended at Calvary. After that first blood-shedding, and not before, He was named JESUS—a Name from first to last connected with Suffering. You know what it means?

J. Yes, Saviour.

Mrs. H. His Name was called Jesus, because "He shall save His people from their sins." He saves all who put their trust in Him from hell too, of course. People often think that the chief part of the deliverance. But you see that is not the way God looks at it. *He* says "*from their sins,*" because He knows that sin is the greatest evil in the universe, and is at the bottom of all suffering, even of hell itself.

Our reading has been a solemn one to-day, dears. But as we are living in a world all spoilt and ruined (for the present) by sin, it is better, isn't it, not to shrink from looking it well in the face? especially as God has found such a Remedy for it; and our worst suffering, if we accept that Remedy, can only be Circumcision, separating us from our sins,—and never the Death* that separates from God.

---

* John v. 24.

Mrs. Hillyard then prayed in these words—

Almighty God, Who madest Thy Blessed Son to be circumcised, and obedient to the law for man; Grant us the true Circumcision of the spirit; that our hearts, and all our members, being mortified from all worldly and carnal lusts, we may in all things obey Thy blessed Will; through the same Thy Son Jesus Christ our Lord.

(*Collect for the Circumcision.*)

THERE is a Name I love to hear,
   I love to speak its worth;
It sounds like music in mine ear,
   The sweetest Name on earth.

It tells me of a Saviour's love,
   Who died to set me free;
It tells me of His precious Blood,
   The sinner's perfect plea.

It tells me of a Father's smile
   Beaming upon His child;
It cheers me through this "little while,"
   Through desert, waste, and wild.

It tells me what my Father hath
   In store for every day,
And though I tread a darksome path,
   Yields sunshine all the way.

It tells of One Whose loving Heart
    Can feel my deepest woe,
Who in my sorrow bears a part
    That none can bear below.

It bids my trembling heart rejoice,
    It dries each rising tear,
It tells me in "a still small voice"
    To trust and never fear.

JESUS ! the Name I love so well,
    The Name I love to hear !
No saint on earth its worth can tell,
    No heart conceive how dear.

This Name shall shed its fragrance still
    Along the thorny road,
Shall sweetly smooth the rugged hill
    That leads me up to God.

And there with all the blood-bought throng,
    From sin and sorrow free,
I'll sing the new eternal song
    Of Jesus' love to me.

                    REV. F. WHITFIELD.

CHAPTER VIII.

THE PRESENTATION IN THE TEMPLE.

Luke ii. 22–39.

ELSIE. Mumsey, I hope we shall have a nicer reading to-day. I didn't like it at all last time, it was all about hurting and killing. I know Jack didn't like it either, though he wouldn't say so. Please make it nicer to-day.

Mrs. Hillyard. Poor little woman, I knew you couldn't understand it, and perhaps if you had understood it you would not have liked it much better, for we never *like* what you call "hurting and killing." But I hope you understood one thing yesterday—that all that Jesus suffered was for *you*, and that He may expect you some day to suffer something for *Him*.

THE PRESENTATION IN THE TEMPLE.

Do you think you could give up anything you liked for Him?

E. Oh yes, I am quite sure I could!

Mrs. H. Well, perhaps, it is better not to say that when you are not asked to do anything you don't like. It is very easy to be brave beforehand. But now we must go on with St. Luke's Gospel. You see I take the events as they occurred, as far as I can, and I don't mean to pick out what you would think the "nice" bits. You would like to know just the *truth* about Jesus, wouldn't you, little one?

E. Yes, Mumsey, I think I should.

Mrs. H. Then now you shall hear the next thing we know about Him, and that is generally called His "Presentation in the Temple." Thirty-three days after Jesus was circumcised, that is to say, when He was about six weeks' old, His parents brought Him to Jerusalem, which you know was the chief city, to present Him to the Lord in the Temple, and to offer a sacrifice there, according to the law of Moses. This was another of the Jewish ceremonial laws, and one which I cannot now explain to you further than this.—You remember that we read in Exodus about the Lord sparing the eldest sons of the Israelites, at the time that He destroyed the first-born of Egypt? Well, He said afterwards that because He had done that, He considered that the Israelites owed their eldest sons to Him, that He had a claim to them; and not only to these children, but also to the first-born of all the animals that they kept, because the first-born of their cattle were also spared in Egypt. If the young animal was what is called in the law a " clean beast," that is, if it was of the sort of animals that were offered in sacrifice, they were to kill it as an offering to the Lord, and when they had burnt the fat (which was considered the best part) upon the altar, and the priest had sprinkled the blood there too, then they might eat the flesh themselves. If it was an unclean animal, such as an ass,* it might be redeemed by a lamb, that is to say, its owner might sacrifice "a lamb without blemish and without spot" in its place, whilst its life was spared; but if he did not

---

* Exod. xiii. 13.

THE PRESENTATION IN THE TEMPLE. 123

think that worth while, then "he must break its neck," without redemption its life was forfeited. In the case of the eldest son of an Israelite, he too, like the " unclean beast," must be redeemed.*

Jack. What an odd law it seems.

Mrs. H. It does. Can you see any typical meaning in it, any of you?

Myles. I suppose that we are like the unclean animals, and can only be saved by a Redeemer.

Mrs. H. Just so, unclean as sinners, and without the Sacrifice of the "Lamb of God" doomed to Eternal Death. But there is another side to it. By offering the first-born of every clean beast, the Israelites bore witness that they held everything from God—their Redeemer, and Deliverer—that they were bound to devote all animal life to the use of Him Who gave it. But the first-born of their children they redeemed. They dared not treat them as they did the animals, for they knew they were made in

---

* The "blood," though not mentioned in the case of the redemption of the first-born of an Israelite, is perhaps implied in Exod. xxxiv. 20, and Num. xviii. 15. If not, then the "redemption" was effected by the payment of money only. See 1 Peter i. 18, 19.

THE HOLY CHILDHOOD.

God's Image, and were therefore to be given to Him in another way than that. But He did want them, and they must be devoted to Him, and this sacrifice bears witness that they belong to Him, and ought to live for Him as a "sacrificed" "consecrated" people.

M. I can't quite see it. That seems as if the children were too bad and unclean to offer to God, and yet too sacred to kill. How can both be true?

Mrs. H. I think both* are true: for man's nature is such a strange combination of the highest and the lowest, the best and the worst, the most precious and the most vile. We are all sacred because we are made in God's Image, and precious to Him, or He would not have paid such a price for us as the Life of His Son. But we have a sinful addition to our original nature, a *graft*, as it were, of evil, which has spoilt us for God's Company, and made us unclean in His Sight. Our very best actions are *dirtied*, so to speak, with sin, and therefore too impure to

---

* For the two aspects of this type, see Maurice's "Doctrine of Sacrifice," p. 56, and Macintosh's "Notes on Exodus" (Morrish).

offer to Him Whom nothing can satisfy but perfect, spotless holiness. Do you see now what I mean?

M. I think I do. People do seem a queer mixture.

Mrs. H. Indeed they do! And then you may as well notice too, that the first-born were but the representatives* of the whole people, which was a holy nation separated for holy uses and services, though they never lived up to their high calling. So also the first-born in Egypt stood for everybody there, for all, Israelites and Egyptians, were under one condemnation, which was only turned aside by the blood on the door-posts.

Christ then, as the first-born of a Jewish mother, but also as the representative of the whole great human family, was brought to the Temple to be presented to the Lord as

---

* "God had taken the tribe of Levi, instead of the first-born (Num. iii. 12), and required only the excess in number of the first-born over the Levites to be redeemed (ib. vers. 44–51). This arrangement appears afterwards to have been superseded by a general command to redeem *all the first-born* at five shekels of the sanctuary" (Num. xviii. 15, 16).—Alford's "N. T. for Eng. Readers," Luke ii. 23.

"holy," which here means *separated*, or *set apart* for "the Lord," and then (although Himself to be the Redeemer of the whole human race), to be redeemed according to God's ordinance. He was the only Man who really lived as man was meant to do, *for God*. So for once, the ceremony of dedication was performed over one who acted it out.

But there was another* law which made it necessary that after the birth of any child, its mother should offer a lamb for a burnt-offering, and a dove or pigeon for a sin-offering; or if she could not afford a lamb, a second dove or young pigeon would do instead. And this was the offering Mary brought, for, as I told you before, she and her husband were poor people. And now, Myles, will you read the rest of our portion for us? It will be verses 25-39.

This passage Myles accordingly read aloud.

Mrs. H. This Temple to which our Lord was brought, was that † which Ezra built after the

---

* Lev. xii.
† Zerubbabel's temple "was still standing in Herod's time, and was more strictly speaking repaired than rebuilt by him."— Smith's "Dict. of the Bible," Art. Temple.

Captivity. Phyllis, read those touching verses in which he describes its foundation being laid.

Phyllis. "But many of the priests and Levites, and chief of the fathers, who were ancient men, that had seen the first house, when the foundation of this house was laid before their eyes, wept with a loud voice; and many shouted aloud for joy; so that the people could not discern the noise of the shout of joy from the noise of the weeping of the people: for the people shouted with a loud shout, and the noise was heard afar off." *

Mrs. H. These old men had great cause for their tears, but if they could have looked on, and seen another old man within that Temple holding in his arms "the Consolation of Israel," they might have been comforted. Why did they cry, Phyllis?

Ph. Because this Temple was not near so grand as the old one.

Mrs. H. My dear child, only the foundation was then laid.

---

* Ezra iii. 12, 13.

Ph. Oh, then they knew it would not be so grand.

Mrs. H. Possibly, but there was a far greater difference between the two Temples than that. Surely, Myles, you know what it was.

M. Well, I declare, I don't think I do, Mother.

Mrs. H. Don't you know what it was that was in the first Temple, that never was in the second until the day when Simeon said "Now lettest Thou Thy servant depart in peace"?

M. Do you mean God's Presence?

Mrs. H. Yes, of course, I do—God is everywhere, but He was present in a special manner in the Holy of Holies; indeed,[*] visibly present in the bright Glory (called the Shekinah) that appeared over the Mercy Seat, though no one but the High Priest ever went in there, and he did only once a year.[†] Didn't you know, Myles, that the Ark of the Covenant—the seat of God's Presence—was never in the second Temple?

M. No, really, I didn't—what became of it then?

---

[*] Lev. xvi. 2.   [†] Heb. ix. 7.

Mrs. H. No one knows what became of it.*
Some people think that before the Jews went
into Captivity they hid it in the wall of Jerusalem, for fear the heathen should seize it, and
that in the excavations now going on there, they
may some day come upon it. But it would
be nothing now but a box—the Glory is
departed. There was a shut-off part of the
second Temple which they called the Holy of
Holies, but that special Presence of the Lord,
which alone could hallow it, was not there.
Therefore Ezra's Temple was a very poor one
compared to Solomon's. The prophet Haggai
says of it, when it was just built—" Who is left
among you that saw this House in her first
glory? and how do ye see it now? is it not in
your eyes in comparison of it as nothing?" ...
And yet he continues, "The glory of this latter
house shall be greater than of the former, saith
the Lord of hosts: and in this place will I give
peace, saith the Lord of hosts." How did He
fulfil that promise, Phyllis?

---

* The legend on this subject in 2 Mac. ii. 4, &c., although
untrustworthy, seems to point to Jeremiah having hidden the
Ark *somewhere*.

Ph. By sending His Son to it.

Mrs. H. Yes. "The Mighty God, the Prince of Peace" came "to His Temple,"* but in a very different way from the triumphal entrance we might have expected. Again, He came "not with observation," yet there were a few souls "looking for Redemption in Jerusalem," who were ready to welcome Him when He did come; God having crowned their faith, and their long waiting, by a revelation of the Holy Ghost, telling them that the Messiah had come. One of these was Simeon—an old man probably, from verse 26. What was the character of Simeon, Jack? We ought to take notice of that, as he was a man so honoured by God.

J. He was "just and devout, waiting for the Consolation of Israel."

Mrs. H. Yes, and what does "just" mean?

J. Fair.

Mrs. H. Yes, and do remember that to be fair is a grand thing. What does it mean, Elsie, when we say—"that isn't fair"?

---

* Mal. iii. 1.

E. O Mumsey! of course I know what that means!

Mrs. H. Yes, my little one, I am sure you do, though you only know one word for it. We all naturally know what "fairness" is, and value it. Jack, you know that if I rewarded Myles, and punished you, you would never dislike me for it, if you were always quite certain that I was *fair* in what I did. And in our games, or our money matters, you know how we value honesty and fair dealing. Everybody does, more or less, I think, even those who steal and cheat themselves, except in countries where people have for centuries degraded themselves, till what remains to be recognised of the Image of God in which we were made, is almost quite rubbed out. We have inherited the love of justice from our Heavenly Father Who values it far more than we can ever do. He delights in calling Himself the "Just" God; and the thought that He could ever fail in His Justice would be unendurable—the most frightful thought, I think, that the heart of man could conceive.

"Just" then, in the way in which Simeon was

"just," means to behave as far as we can, faithfully and fairly towards each other, but it means much more than that. It means being "just with God." How can we be that, Phyllis?

Ph. By believing in Jesus.

Mrs. H. Yes, when we come to desire to be "just with God,"—that means so perfectly to have fulfilled all our obligations to *Him*,* as to satisfy His requirements,—we find that the only way to do that is to take shelter in Jesus, His "Righteous Servant," Who "shall justify many." We can't ever be good enough to please God any other way. But in our Surety He sees us to be "without fault." We are "accepted in the Beloved." But Simeon got beyond being "just," even as regarded God. What was he besides?

J. "Devout."

Mrs. H. Yes, he was "just" first, and "devout" after. One of the most disgusting forms of hypocrisy, or self-deceit, is when what seems like devotion is not founded upon justice. There have been people who were praying for their

---

* Luke x. 27.

neighbours at meetings, and cheating them all the time.

M. What awful humbugs!

Mrs. H. No doubt; the worst of it is, that such people often humbug themselves as well as others, and think that somehow they are all right—I mean right as to getting off punishment, they don't want to be rid of sin.

Ph. But how can they imagine they are Christians, Mother?

Mrs. H. Partly I think through bad teaching: they may have heard continually that God offers a free pardon to sinners, and that whosoever believes in Christ is safe for ever, and because they believe these truths as doctrines, they fancy that they are trusting *Christ;* and nobody has ever plainly told them that they are going to hell; and that is what they want. Instead of that, because they have got up a certain kind of cant, and can talk about "the Lord's people," "saving faith," and so forth, they are too often considered to be all right. These expressions do duty for the real thing!

M. I suppose you think that any one who

really was a Christian could not ever steal or cheat?

Mrs. H. I should be afraid to say that, Myles; but I do say that if a true Christian had fallen into such a sin he would lose all that fellowship with God which alone can make true devotion possible, until by His grace he was restored again ; and I say too that it would be perfectly impossible that he could live in habitual dishonesty. Suppose, for instance, that a grocer who professed to be a believer in the Lord Jesus Christ, was using false weights and measures in his shop, such a man ought never to be considered in any sense of the word a Christian, however he might talk about "Justification by Faith," and "Imputed Righteousness." Indeed I should say there was no Gospel for him as long as he was determined to go on cheating his customers. God said plainly to this same class of people in the days of the prophet Micah, "Shall I count them pure with the wicked balances, and with the bag of deceitful weights?"* And how could He? for the

---

* Micah vi. 11.

Gospel is not a kind of contrivance by which we can keep our sins and yet be saved from punishment. It is just the reverse of that. Its end and object is to produce the greatest possible amount of goodness, and God knew that it would effect that purpose, for it supplies the strongest, and purest, and most unselfish motive for right conduct—grateful love, as well as the power to act upon that motive.

Ph. Yes, of course, but you couldn't go and tell the grocer he was going to hell and all that, unless you had found him out.

Mrs. H. Certainly not! but with sounder teaching there would not be many such characters. There will always be some false brethren no doubt, for one of our Lord's Apostles was a thief, but such teaching as the Sermon on the Mount, and some of Christ's thundering denunciations of the "hypocrites who devour widows' houses, and for a pretence make long prayers," would clear out most of them pretty fast, I fancy, from amongst Christians, if they were not converted.

But we have strayed away eighteen centuries

from Simeon! Tell me, lastly, Jack, what this dear old man was waiting for?

J. Christ.

Mrs H. Yes; when God's children are truly just, and truly devout, then they begin to long for the Coming of Jesus. Verses 34 and 35 are rather difficult—what do you think they mean, Myles?

M. Didn't Christ say He was a "stone of stumbling" to the Jews?

Mrs. H. He did, and in St. Peter's 1st Epistle, 2d chapter, and 7th and 8th verses, you will find the same thing. It means that they were too proud to accept Jesus of Nazareth as their Messiah, and that their rejection of Him sunk them deeper in guilt than ever they were. That, as I understand it at least, is the "fall" here spoken of. The "rising again," I think, refers to the faithful remnant of true Israelites who will yet accept their King, and through whose ministry, as His subjects, great blessing will come upon the heathen world.* I am

---

* Rom. xi. 11, 12, 15.

THE PRESENTATION IN THE TEMPLE. 137

speaking now of things in the future, which we can only dimly guess at by the light of prophecy.

M. Well then, about the "sign which shall be spoken against"—what does that mean, do you think, Mother?

Mrs. H. Why did I tell you Jesus was called "The Word"?

M. Because He came to express God's Thoughts.

Mrs. H. And He revealed *man's* thoughts too. Before He came, the ungodly hated God, as they always did, and do still. Men in their natural, unrenewed state, are at enmity with God—the hatred being all on their side. But though they hated Him, they had no way of openly showing their hatred. Many of them were hypocrites, and pretended to love Him, and thought they did perhaps. But when God was manifest in the flesh—in their midst—their hatred broke out into action, and they killed Him. Their "thoughts" were "revealed" then.

"They scorned Him for His Goodness,
That world of evil men,—
And if He came to England
'Twould be just the same again!

"They made up their minds to kill Him
And get Him out of their sight,
For the sinful hates the Holy,
And darkness hates the Light."

We need not wonder, then, that a sword should pass through His mother's heart! She, like her Son, was deeply "acquainted with grief." And what may have added bitterness to her sorrow was, that probably she never fully understood His Mission upon earth until He had left it.

E. You haven't told us anything about the old woman, Anna, Mother.

Mrs. H. There is no more to tell, dear, than St. Luke has told us. She was a Prophetess, and no doubt one who, like Simeon, was "just and devout," and she was "looking for redemption in Israel" as several others were—looking for Jesus, that is. But she expected Him because she prayed for His Coming so much; she used to be praying and fasting night and day in the Temple. When God means to "visit His people," and to bless them in some great way, He always raises up a band of praying people beforehand. That is the way He does things.

He never sends a great blessing without much prayer. But though Anna was so much occupied in prayer, and was such a very old woman, she yet had time to "speak" of the Redeemer she expected, and she and her friends had more praise than prayer after that day that she and Simeon welcomed the Blessed Child in His Temple.

Almighty and everlasting God, we humbly beseech Thy Majesty, that as Thy only-begotten Son was presented in the Temple in substance of our flesh, so we may be presented unto Thee with pure and clean hearts, by the same Thy Son Jesus Christ our Lord. Amen.
Collect for the Purification of B. V. Mary.

> COME, let us search our hearts, and try
> If all our ways be right :
> Is God's great rule of equity
> Our practice and delight?
>
> Have we to others truly done,
> As we would have them do?
> Envious, unkind, and false to none ;
> But always just and true?

In vain we speak of Jesus' Blood,
   And place in Him our trust,
If while we boast our love to God,
   We prove to men unjust.

Thou, before Whom we stand in awe,
   And tremble and obey,
Write in our hearts Thy perfect law,
   And keep us in Thy way.
WATTS.

CHAPTER IX.

THE STAR IN THE EAST.

MATT. II. 1-10.

JACK and Elsie appeared rather subdued next morning, though no one but their mother noticed it; and when she asked God's Blessing on their study of His Word, she did so with a very thankful heart.

Shall I tell you what had happened? If I do, I must let you a little way into Elsie's secrets, but it won't be wrong to do that as she is not a real little girl; though I daresay you will think that the story is not worth telling.

The evening after the Reading last recorded, Mrs. Hillyard had sat waiting for some time in her dressing-room, before dinner, expecting Elsie to come and say her little prayer, and wish her good-night. Usually she ran upstairs as fast as she could to "help" her father or mother dress for dinner, and when that ceremony had been performed, with her valuable assistance, and she had blown soap-bubbles in her father's basin, over-scented his pocket handkerchief, and stuck a flower in his buttonhole; or when she had rendered her mother services of a similar nature, she was accustomed to say her hymn and her prayer in her mother's room, and as soon as the gong sounded, go off to bed.

On this occasion, however, Mrs. Hillyard had finished dressing, and yet no Elsie appeared. Having ascertained that she was not with her father, she sent her maid to the nursery to fetch her, and even then it was some minutes before she came reluctantly into the room. At that moment the gong sounded for dinner, and Elsie hurriedly wished her mother good-night, and saying that it was now too late for her prayers, would have run away. But Mrs. Hillyard saw there was something wrong, and called her back, and then taking her on her knee asked her what was the matter? At first the poor little girl would not speak, but after hesitating a minute, she asked,

"Saying one's prayers is being devout, isn't it?"

Mrs. Hillyard could hardly help laughing at the quaintness of the question. She forgot at the moment the conversation they had had that morning about Simeon, and she answered as gravely as she could,

"That depends, little one, if people really pray when they say their prayers—that is devotion, certainly."

"And if they don't really pray, then it's no good at all?"

"No, I don't think it is any good."

"Then, Mumsey, don't ask me why, but I won't say my prayers to-night please."

Mrs. Hillyard suddenly remembered then what she had told her children about uprightness coming before devotion, and, with a throb of great thankfulness to Almighty God that her teaching was bearing upon their practice, she inquired,

"My poor little darling, you have done something wrong, haven't you?"

"Yes," answered Elsie, bursting into tears.

"Tell me, dear, is it against any person, or is it against God alone?"

"It's Jack—I cheated him yesterday," sobbed Elsie.

"Oh dear! I am grieved that you could have done that, but I am very glad you are so sorry."

"I'll tell you what it was, Mother, I——"

"Stop, Elsie! don't tell *me* what you did, but run away and tell Jack, and make it all square with him, and ask him to forgive you, and then come back to me for your prayers."

Elsie had to run into the garden to find Jack, but it was not very long before she returned, saying the affair was all settled and that Jack was not a bit angry.

Then the little girl asked God's Pardon and Help, and thanked Him that Jesus had died for her sins, and if ever in her little life she had prayed with all her heart, she did so that evening; and she laid down, feeling as sure of the forgiveness of her Heavenly Father as she did of her mother's, when she came upstairs afterwards to give her a last kiss. Still she felt very unhappy that she should have been so naughty.

No more was ever heard of it of course, but Jack was more patronising to her than usual for a day or two, and next time he went to Huxley he bought her a pop-gun for a present.

But we must now return to the Bible Reading.

Mrs. H. To-day you will have a story you all of you know quite well, told by St. Matthew. Possibly it may some of it have happened before the Presentation in the Temple, but the end must have happened after that. St. Luke never mentions it at all; you remember he ended the account of the visit to Jerusalem by saying, "And when they had performed all things according to the law of the Lord, they returned into Galilee, to their own city Nazareth." And yet here we find Joseph and Mary apparently living at Bethlehem, and Matthew never says a word about their having been at Jerusalem. I can't explain how that is—nobody can; but no doubt if we could ask Matthew and Luke, they could put it straight for us in two minutes, by relating other facts which neither had written down.

K

J. Who was Matthew, Mother?

Mrs. H. By trade he was a tax-gatherer to the Romans, before he was called to be an Apostle. He may possibly have been a first cousin of our Lord's, but I am inclined to think he was not. Two of his brothers were Apostles besides himself.

Mrs. Hillyard then read the second chapter of Matthew.

Mrs. H. And now, Elsie, tell me—Who was King of Judea when Jesus was born?

E. A horrid, bad man, called Herod.

Mrs. H. That's right, Elsie! He was called Herod the Great, but he was one of the most infamous wretches that ever lived—something, Myles, like some of the worst of the Roman Emperors, in later days.

M. Really,—why on earth did they call him "Great," then? because he was a great brute?

Mrs. H. He certainly had no higher claim to greatness, though to please the Jews, who hated him, he had magnificently restored the Temple and was liberal with his money in other ways. He had no sort of right to the throne which he had seized, with the assistance of the

Romans, about thirty years before the birth of Christ. He was a strange mixture of races, for though he had adopted the Jews' religion, his ancestors had ever been their bitterest enemies, his father being an Edomite, and his mother an Ishmaelite, whilst all his own ideas of government, and of enjoyment, he had borrowed from the Romans or the Greeks.* Now then, Phyllis, who were the Edomites?

Ph. The descendants of Esau.

Mrs. H. Quite right; and Jack, who was Herod's mother's ancestor, Ishmael?

J. I know—he was Hagar's son, and used to quarrel with Isaac.

Mrs. H. Yes. Esau and Ishmael were wild enough ancestors to have, but Herod was a thousand times worse than either of them. And now, Elsie, I must ask you another question— Who came to see Herod, at Jerusalem, soon after Jesus was born?

E. Some wise men from the East.

Mrs. H. Yes. They seem to have come from a long way off, and most probably were astrologers.

---

* See Farrar's "Life of Christ," vol. i. p. 25.

Ph. What are astrologers, Mother? are they anything like astronomers?

Mrs. H. So far that both get their name from the stars, they are—but astrologers were men who made a study of the stars with the idea that they could tell people's fortunes, and even find out what great events were going to happen, from the signs they observed in the heavens. People were very ignorant in those days, and no one doubted that astrology was a great science. Astrologers were still called "wise men" in the East, just as they were in Daniel's time.* You remember how Nebuchadnezzar sent for them to tell his dream?

M. Yes; but, Mother, I tell you what I never can make out. These men saw some wonderful "Star" in their own country, and they saw it again after they left Herod, they don't seem to have seen it between. Then what made them hit upon Jerusalem, of all places in the world, to go to? and what made them tell Herod about the "King of the Jews" being born?—how could they have known that?

---

* Dan. ii. 12, 14, 18, 24, &c.

THE HOMAGE OF THE MAGI.

THE STAR IN THE EAST.

Ph. God told them in a dream, didn't He, Mother?

Mrs. H. Not that we know of. There seems to have been a general expectation at that time that some great King was coming. I see in this book* here, that a Roman historian, Suetonius, wrote (about 100 years after Christ's Birth),—"that there prevailed an ancient and consistent opinion in all the East, that it was fated that at that time those should go forth from Judea who should rule the Empire:" and that Tacitus (another historian) mentions the same circumstance in almost the same words. Now both these men had the greatest contempt for the Christians—so they didn't say this to serve their cause in any way. A Jewish historian, Josephus, says the same thing. Perhaps, also, in the East, traditions may have still lingered about the "Star" that another † wise man there had spoken of in prophecy. I mean Balaam, who was also an Eastern astrologer. And again (which is, I think, more to the point than anything else that we know on the subject),

---

* Dean Alford's "New Testament for English Readers."
† Num. xxiv. 17.

150   THE HOLY CHILDHOOD.

the Prophet Daniel, 600 years before, had been made, by the great Sovereign of the East, head over all the Babylonian "wise men;"* and his teaching respecting "the Messiah the Prince," † Who was to come, could hardly fail to be handed down to his successors, who would then be expecting this great Event.

M. Mother, what do you think the Star was, that they saw?

Mrs. H. Well, it is a most interesting fact that there was just about this very time, three times, indeed ‡ in one year, a conjunction of the planets Jupiter and Saturn (that is an apparent meeting together of these two stars) and that soon after they were joined by the planet Mars. When the same conjunction occurred in 1603–1604 A.D., it was accompanied by the appearance of a very large and brilliant star, which after shining for a whole year, gradually disappeared. One of these conjunctions of Jupiter and Saturn, the Eastern astrologers may have seen in their own country, and afterwards, another, when they had left Jerusalem, and

---
* Dan. ii. 48.   † Dan. ix. 25.
‡ Farrar's "Life of Christ," vol. i. p. 31.

were on their way to Bethlehem. It is of course possible, and even probable, that an evanescent (or vanishing) star accompanied the strange appearances, as in 1604, but this cannot now be ascertained. One more remarkable fact about them *is*, however, ascertained— Do you know what the constellations are, Jack?

J. Yes, I know the Great Bear quite well. Father showed it me.

Ph. And I know Orion, and the Pleiades, too.

Mrs. H. Well then, there is another called Pisces, or the Fish, and any remarkable appearance in it was always supposed by astrologers to have something to do with Judea. Now the astronomer Kepler calculated that the three conjunctions which, as I have told you, occurred in one year, about the time Christ was born, were visible in this particular constellation, and not again, in it, for 794 years.

M. What an extraordinary thing!

Mrs. H. It is, isn't it! and very interesting too, being, indeed, quite sufficient to account for their turning their steps towards Jerusalem.

Ph. Then you don't think it was a miracle, Mother?

Mrs. H. It seems to me more likely that it was not: of course it may have been, and in that case it was best so, for God never makes mistakes. Therefore, it may be a foolish feeling on my part, but I confess I should be rather disappointed if it were proved to have been a miracle. It seems to give us such a wonderful view of God's Almighty Power and Wisdom, that what we call the "ordinary laws of nature," working with their usual regularity, and even the ignorant superstitions of men, should meet together to fulfil His Will with such Divine exactness. God seems always to have been sparing of what we call "miracles," even in days when it was necessary to work some.

M. But if the Star went before them till it stood over a particular house, it must surely have been a miracle?

Mrs. H. Yes, it must—but no house is mentioned. The road they had to take from Jerusalem to Bethlehem, lay probably in the direction of this bright light, or "Star," and when they reached the village it was shining over it, or perhaps some part of it. And now we must go on. Herod, you see, being a usurper, and a foreigner, was naturally alarmed at hearing of a rival who was *born* King of the Jews. You remember the announcement of the angel Gabriel to the Blessed Virgin, that "the Lord God should give unto Jesus the Throne of His father David:" and that "He shall reign over the house of Jacob for ever; and of His kingdom there shall be no end"? And you know that Pontius Pilate put as a title over His Cross, "The King of the Jews"?

Ph. Yes, but He never was really a king.

Mrs. H. He never reigned as a king on earth, because the Jews rejected Him. They said "We will not have this man to reign over us!" "We have no king but Cæsar!" But the days will yet come when a remnant of them will humble themselves before Him, and will accept Him as their Sovereign.

Ph. And what will happen then, Mother?

Mrs. H. Then He Himself will reign over His people Israel at Jerusalem.

Ph. Do you mean *really?*

Mrs. H. I mean *really.*

Ph. But when will that be?

Mrs. H. When He comes again to this world.

I can't tell you *when*, but I hope and think that it may be soon.

Ph. But, Mother, is it really in the Bible that He is coming on earth to reign like a King?

Mrs. H. Have we not just read it in Luke i. 33?—it is said in many other places too. Why should you find it so difficult to believe?

Ph. I don't know—only it seems so wonderful.

Mrs. H. It would be more wonderful, I think, if He did not come, when God has so plainly told us that He would.

M. But, Mother, supposing the Jews had crowned Him King, when He came before, how would He have died for our sins?

Mrs. H. I don't know.

M. He *must* have died, mustn't He?

Mrs. H. Yes, "Christ must needs have suffered." *

M. Well then, how would it have been?

Mrs. H. I tell you, my boy, I don't know. There is never any information given in the Bible, that I can see, as to how things might

---

* Acts xvii. 3.

have been arranged that never happened. You might as well ask what would have happened had Adam and Eve never sinned, the "Lamb" having been "slain from the foundation of the world." They did sin, and so did the Jews. —But, Elsie, you poor little patient thing, it is too bad our talking about astrology and astronomy at your Bible lesson, and then trying to settle about what isn't in the Bible at all. You may run away if we behave like that another time.

E. O Mumsey! I was quite happy, I was playing with Kitty.

Mrs. H. Now Jack shall tell us the story—and you listen, Elsie, and pull him up if he makes any mistakes—you and Jack always get on splendidly when you are set to mind each other. Go on, Jack, from where "Herod was troubled, and all Jerusalem with him."

J. Well, then, he called a lot of people and asked them where Christ should be born, and they said at Bethlehem, because it was in the Bible.

Mrs. H. Where, in the Bible?

J. Oh, I don't know.

Mrs. H. It is in the book of Micah (chap. v. ver. 2), and I should like to observe in this place that " CHRIST " means the *Lord's Anointed One.* Kings, you know, were anointed with oil. I also wish to say that Herod, bad man though he was, and the "priests and scribes," though they were not much better, had a very much clearer notion of how to interpret prophecy than most scholars have had since. They believed that prophecy was intended by God to guide, rather than to mislead, those that study it; and so, as Micah had said that the Ruler in Israel should "come forth from Bethlehem," to Bethlehem the sages were despatched. Go on, Jack.

J. Herod asked the wise men how long ago they had seen the Star. Was that to find out how old Jesus was, Mother?

Mrs. H. I suppose so.

J. And then he told them to go and hunt about for the young child, and come back and tell him, as soon as ever they had found Him, that he might go and worship Him too. Of course that was only a dodge—he never meant to go. But the wise men believed him, I suppose,

and off they went, and when they had started —there was the Star again! and they were awfully pleased at seeing it again, and went on towards it till they got to Bethlehem. And that's all.

Mrs. H. Yes, that is all, and you got through without Elsie's assistance! Next time we shall finish the story, and find that these ignorant but faithful men were well enough rewarded for their long journey—for they found Jesus at the end of it!

O God, Who by the leading of a star didst manifest Thy only-begotten Son to the Gentiles; Mercifully grant, that we, which know Thee now by faith, may after this life have the fruition of Thy glorious Godhead; through Jesus Christ our Lord. Amen.
(*Collect for the Epiphany.*)

Hail to the Lord's Anointed,
  Great David's greater Son!
Hail, in the time appointed,
  His reign on earth begun!
He comes to break oppression,
  To set the captive free,
To take away transgression,
  And rule in equity.

He shall come down like showers
  Upon the fruitful earth,
And joy and hope, like flowers,
  Spring in His path to birth:
Before Him on the mountains
  Shall peace, the herald, go;
From hill to vale the fountains
  Of righteousness o'erflow.

Kings shall bow down before Him,
  And gold and incense bring;
All nations shall adore Him,
  His praise all people sing;
To Him shall prayer unceasing
  And daily vows ascend;
His Kingdom still increasing,
  A Kingdom without end.

O'er every foe victorious
  He on His throne shall rest;
From age to age more glorious,
  All blessing and all blessed:
The tide of time shall never
  His covenant remove;
His Name shall stand for ever,
  His changeless Name of Love.

JAMES MONTGOMERY.

CHAPTER X.

"*THE KING OF THE JEWS.*"

MATT. II. 11-23.

HEN Mrs. Hillyard had slowly read the rest of the second chapter of Matthew, she said—
"I think you would all have understood this passage, with the exception of the quotations from the Old Testament, even if you had not known the story so well before."

Phyllis. How far was Bethlehem from Jerusalem, Mother?

Mrs. Hillyard. About six miles, I think.

Jack. Mother, don't you think the wise men must have been surprised to find that after all Jesus was only a poor person's baby? Do you think they expected Him to be very grand?

Mrs. H. Perhaps they did, dear; but they had been guided by God's "sure word of prophecy,"* and had been faithful to the light it gave them; and so He gave them more light, and faith enough to believe that "Jesus is Lord"† in spite of His appearing with no worldly grandeur. And surely we may learn a great lesson here, by contrasting their spirit in at once receiving and acting upon the very small part of God's Word which had been given them—with that of the chief priests and scribes, who were so ready with their Biblical information — spotting their text in Micah, without a moment's hesitation, and yet never dreaming of accompanying the wise men in their search for Him of whom their prophets testified. Not they!—On the contrary, they, with "all Jerusalem," were "troubled" at the very thought of such a disturbing, inconvenient discovery, as that would be. It would put them out altogether, and disarrange all their time-serving policy to find the true "King of the Jews." Far better let Him be quietly put out

---

* 2 Peter i. 19. † 1 Cor. xii. 3.

of the way by Herod "the Great," whilst they, of course, knew nothing about it! And all this time they were no doubt as keen as could be about their religious controversies, and ready to tear each other's eyes out over their trumpery disputes about words.

Myles. What wretches! they were worse than Herod himself.

Mrs. H. In some respects perhaps they were, for they were more responsible. But do let us remember that their hearts were no worse than ours, and that it is an awful responsibility for *us* to know much of the Bible. If it doesn't lead us to seek for Jesus, and to find *Him*, it would be far better for us never to have opened it,—far better to have learnt from the old heathens as much goodness as they could teach us, than a system of doctrines about Christ, that never leads us to Himself. The Bible has taught many people *all about* Jesus, to whom He will yet declare at the last that *He* never knew *them*. But don't let this frighten you, dear children, as long as you have the smallest wish really to find out God's Will, and to do it, when you read the Bible, you can't

L

be misusing it. Has any one any question to ask?

Ph. Yes, I have; I want to know whether the Bible says anywhere that there were three wise men. I thought it did, but I can't find it.

Mrs. H. Oh no; we are never told how many there were; in pictures there are generally three, but there is no good reason for believing that.

M. I always thought there were three of them, because they brought three presents— gold, and frankincense, and myrrh.

Mrs. H. You may be right, dear, but I don't see myself that necessarily they each gave one thing.

J. Is there anything else about them in the Bible, Mother?

Mrs. H. Nothing whatever. One can't help wondering what became of them, and whether they lived to hear that the Jews had crucified their King.

M. Do you think that Herod ever found out that he had not killed Jesus?

Mrs. H. No, I shouldn't think so. The poor miserable man was actually dying at the very time he was committing these murders to secure his throne, and he must even then have been suffering agonies of pain from the loathsome disease of which he died in a few weeks, or months at the farthest.

But pain often seems to make wicked people more wicked: they get desperate under it, I suppose, when they have hardened their hearts against God. Herod had strangled his wife, drowned his brother-in-law (who was then High Priest), murdered his own three sons, his uncle, his stepmother, the father, and the uncle of his wife, his cousin, and two of his friends—besides numbers more. He had burnt, cut in two, strangled, and secretly assassinated his victims. He had tortured others like a fiend, and five days before his death attempted, but failed, to kill himself. He died the most horrible and agonising death possible to a human being, for like a future namesake of his, he was eaten by worms whilst he was still alive. This took place at Jericho, where he had gone six weeks before for the sake of the baths. The thought of the general rejoicing which he felt sure would be made at his death, enraged him so much that he determined, if possible, to turn it into mourning; he therefore commanded—and this was the very last act of his life—that under pain of death all the chiefs of the tribes, and of the great families of Judea, should come to Jericho. They did come, and were shut up by his orders in one large building; he then secretly commanded his sister that the moment he died they should all be killed. However they were not, but the day of his death was, as he was afraid it would be, kept as a great holiday.*

J. Why he must have been as bad as the devil!

Mrs. H. I don't think there could be much to choose between them. But is it not awful to see what human nature may come to!

M. It is indeed!

Mrs. H. All these notorious crimes of Herod's made the Bethlehem massacre seem a very small affair. The slaughter of a dozen or two babies in a small Jewish town and its "coasts" (which here means outskirts) was not thought worth recording by any of the writers of the day,

---

* Farrar's "Life of Christ," vol. i. pp. 42-48.

even if they knew of it—by those at least whose writings have been preserved—and yet it seems in one way to have been the worst of any of his crimes—not for its brutality chiefly, for some of the others were still more brutal— but because of its daring impiety. Herod believed the Jewish Scriptures, and yet no sooner was he convinced that the Messiah Whom God had promised, and Whom he himself called "Christ," was really come, than he did his best to murder Him.

Ph. How dreadful it seems!

Mrs. H. Doesn't it? And remember this was a man who was religious in some ways. It is stated that the Emperor Augustus said of him, on hearing of his assassination of one of his sons, that "it was better to be Herod's pig than his son." He meant that his pig would be pretty safe, as it would be *against his conscience* (as a Jewish proselyte) *to eat pork*, though not to murder his children. But let us take leave of this monster—there are some other points we must talk about, but as you two little ones won't be able to understand this part, you had better run away and teach each other as much of this pretty

hymn as you can learn whilst we are finishing
our reading—

> " Saw you never in the twilight,
>   When the sun had left the skies,
> Up in heaven the clear stars shining,
>   Through the gloom like silver eyes?
> So of old the wise men watching,
>   Saw a little stranger star,
> And they knew the King was given,
>   And they followed it from far.
>
> " Heard you never of the story,
>   How they crossed the desert wild,
> Journeyed on by plain and mountain,
>   Till they found the Holy Child?
> How they opened all their treasures,
>   Kneeling to that Infant King,
> Gave the gold and fragrant incense,
>   Gave the myrrh in offering?
>
> " Know ye not that lowly Baby
>   Was the Bright and Morning Star,
> He Who came to light the Gentiles,
>   And the darkened Isles afar?
> And we too may seek His cradle,
>   There our heart's best treasures bring,
> Love, and Faith, and true Devotion,
>   For our Saviour, God, and King."' *

* Mrs. Alexander.

THE KING OF THE JEWS. 167

Mrs. Hillyard then continued—"I want you to notice that Matthew's Gospel is much more Jewish than either of the others. Almost every sentence he writes has some reference to his nation—he seems never to have had it out of his head for a minute. His Gospel was specially God's message to Israel, and sets Jesus forth peculiarly as their Messiah. That is why it begins straight away with the Jewish genealogy of Joseph—why such a point is made of Jesus being 'born King of the Jews'—and why there are such continual quotations from the Old Testament, and references to it. To bring out these prophecies, and to show the Old Testament to have been ever, from end to end, pointing to Christ, seems to have been Matthew's particular work, though it was also the work, only not so peculiarly, of the other Evangelists.

"Now remember he had in his mind that Jesus was to reign one day at Jerusalem, and that the peace and prosperity of Solomon's reign, with all its magnificence, was but a typical foreshadowing of the glories of the Kingdom of Christ, and that thus it was a first and partial fulfilment of the earlier promises. In Solomon's reign, for the only period in Israel's history, their enemies were subdued, and they had dominion over the whole land of Canaan, with its proper boundaries, as it had been given by promise to Abraham.* Turn to Psalm 72, Myles, and you will see that though said to be 'for Solomon,' the heading at the top of the page rightly describes it as 'Messiah's Reign.'

"It applied, in fact, to both—to the immediate reign of Solomon, but more to the future Kingdom of Christ. Will you read it through?"

Myles did so, but when he got to the 11th verse he said—"Why this is just like the wise men, Mother, only that they weren't kings, I suppose."

Mrs. H. I hoped you would observe that—but go on.

Myles finished the Psalm, and then remarked—"And there was the 'gold' too, that they brought—in the 15th verse—how curious!"

Mrs. H. Yes, it seems as if the wise men in bringing their tribute of homage from the East, to the Infant King, were, without knowing

---

* Gen. xv. 18; Josh. i. 4; Ps. lxxii. 8; 1 Kings iv. 21-24; Zech. ix. 10.

it, proclaiming Jesus to be the great anti-type of Solomon, Who would receive, in that very land, the homage of all the kings of the earth. It was a little passing glimpse, as it were, even then—or as we may say a rehearsal—of his future sovereignty, and a recognition of it on the part of God. The "gold" was very likely a symbol of royalty here, as in other places in Scripture.

Ph. What were the frankincense and myrrh for?

Mrs. H. Frankincense was used as a perfume: one can perhaps understand their bringing that as a present; and it reminds one of the sweet ointment, "very precious," with which women afterwards anointed His Head and His Feet. But myrrh was a very bitter sort of gum; why they brought that it is impossible to say, though it *may* have shown, as in a parable (of course without their knowing it) the bitter cup that Jesus had to drink before He could "receive for Himself a Kingdom, and return" to reign.

But we should look at the references to Old Testament prophecies before we close. They are very difficult to understand.

M. I was just looking at Hosea xi. 1, but I can't make out how it applies to Christ.

Mrs. H. No writers on prophecy now would ever have dreamt of applying it to Him, I am sure, if St. Matthew had not done so. But he does, and by doing so shows us how much more full the Old Testament is of Christ than we should ever think. You see it was written by One to Whom he was All in All, and everything connected with Israel, of whom the Lord had said to Pharaoh, "Israel is My Son, My first-born," * was in His Mind connected with Christ, the "Beloved Son in Whom" He is "well pleased." Israel had been called to show forth nationally what Christ did show forth personally—"Holiness to the Lord." How utterly they failed, and how completely He—the true Israel—succeeded, we know in a measure. Have I at all explained it to you?

M. I think the verse in Exodus does explain it a little.

Ph. I have a kind of an idea, I think, of what you mean, Mother.

Mrs. H. And I have only "a kind of an idea"

* Ex. iv. 22.

THE KING OF THE JEWS. 171

of what St. Matthew means by any of his quotations in this chapter, so we must be satisfied without any clearer explanations of them for the present. Rachel, Jacob's wife, was buried close to Bethlehem; but why Jeremiah introduces her into his prophecy of the Babylonian captivity, and why Matthew brings in that prophecy here, it is not easy to say. Rachel, no doubt, represents poetically the mothers of Israel, who were again bereaved at Bethlehem, and that is as much as I understand of the passage.*

As to the last verse, it is far the most satisfactory explanation of it, I think, that the title "Nazarene" † is derived from the Hebrew word *Nazir*, so that it would be better rendered *Nazirean*, than Nazarene. That word means "separation"—either in the sense of being dedi-

---

* "Jer. xxxi. 15 applied originally to the captivity. In this quotation also St. Matthew has translated freely from the Hebrew original. The remark of Calvin, that 'Matthew *does not mean that the prophet had predicted what Herod should do*, but that, at the advent of Christ, that mourning was renewed which many years before the women of Bethlehem had made,' is characterised by his usual strong and honest common sense, and must be borne in mind in considering several of the gospel references to ancient prophecy."—Farrar's "Life of Christ," vol. i. p. 41.

† See Lightfoot's Works, vol. xi. p. 44. (Ed. 1823.)

cated to God, as the *Nazarites* were, or merely as being despised and cast out by men. In this last sense the word is used in Gen. xlix. 26.—read it, Phyllis.

Ph. " The blessings of thy father .... shall be on the head of Joseph, and on the crown of the head of him that was separate from his brethren."

Mrs. H. Yes. And you see Matthew gives as his authority for this prophecy, not one prophet, but all—"which was spoken by the prophets." Now all the prophets bore witness to the fact that the Messiah would be "despised and rejected of men," but not one of them ever said—not at least in any book now existing—that He would live at Nazareth. Still, the town no doubt derived its name from *Nazir*, on account of its having always been an unpopular place; therefore it was specially fitted, and specially chosen, as the home of the despised Jesus. It is curious to find that even a thousand years before Christ, the cities of Galilee had already got such a bad name, that when Solomon made a present of twenty of them to Hiram, King of Tyre, in consideration, I suppose, of his having supplied him with timber and gold for the building of the Temple; instead of being obliged to him, he seems to have felt quite insulted, for he said—"What cities are those which thou hast given me? And he called them the land of Cabul unto this day;"* and Cabul means *disgusting*.

M. How the things in the Bible seem to fit one into the other.

Mrs. H. Don't they! You will find more and more what a wonderful Book it is, if you only *study* it. People who have really done that prayerfully may often come to parts they can't understand at all, but as long as they are walking according to its precepts, they can scarcely ever have their confidence in its being God's Word shaken in the least.

O Almighty God, Who out of the mouths of babes and sucklings hast ordained strength: and madest infants to glorify Thee by their deaths; Mortify and kill all vices in us, and so strengthen us by Thy grace, that by the innocency of our lives, and constancy of our faith even unto death, we may glorify Thy Holy Name; through Jesus Christ our Lord. Amen.

(*Collect for The Innocents' Day.*)

---

* 1 Kings ix. 11–13.

As with gladness men of old
Did the guiding star behold,
As with joy they hailed its light,
Leading onward, beaming bright;
So, most gracious Lord, may we
Ever more be led to Thee.

As with joyful steps they sped,
Saviour, to thy lowly bed,
There to bend the knee before
Thee Whom Heaven and earth adore;
So may we with willing feet
Ever seek Thy mercy seat.

As they offered gifts most rare
At Thy cradle rude and bare;
So may we with holy joy,
Pure and free from sin's alloy,
All our costliest treasures bring,
Christ, to Thee our Heavenly King.

Holy Jesus, every day
Keep us in the narrow way;
And, when earthly things are past,
Bring our ransomed souls at last
Where they need no Star to guide,
Where no clouds Thy Glory hide.

In the heavenly country bright,
Need they no created light;
Thou its Light, its Joy, its Crown,
Thou its Sun Which goes not down;
There for ever may we sing
Alleluias to our King!

Hymns Ancient and Modern.

CHAPTER XI.

THE PASSOVER.

Luke ii. 40-42.

ELSIE. Mother, I do so want to come to where Jesus is a little Boy.

Mrs. Hillyard. We shall come to that to-day; but I am afraid you will be disappointed to hear that there is only one story about Him when He was a Child, in the whole Bible. That we shall begin to-day.

E. Oh, I am so sorry! I wanted to hear ever so much about Him when He was little.

Mrs. H. We should all have liked to hear more, of course, but it is better for us to know no more than we do, or God would have told us more. All that He has thought fit to tell us about the Childhood of Jesus, from His

Infancy till He was twelve years old, we find in the 40th verse of the 2nd chapter of Luke, where we begin our reading this morning, 'The Child grew, and waxed strong, becoming filled with wisdom: and the grace of God was upon Him.' *

He grew bodily, just as you children grow, in age and stature, and He also 'waxed strong in spirit' by becoming gradually filled with wisdom.

Mrs. Hillyard then read Luke ii. 41, 42.

Mrs. H. Do either of you little ones know what the Feast of the Passover was?

Jack. Yes, I do; the Jews kept it in remembrance of the time when their eldest boys were saved from being killed in Egypt.

Mrs. H. Yes; but it was God's commandment that they should keep it, not their own idea. There were two other feasts to which He ordered all the men to go up to Jerusalem—Pentecost, and Tabernacles. Women were not obliged to go to any of the feasts, but a great many did go up once a year to the Passover. Mary, you

---

* Alford's translation.

THE PASSOVER.

see, went with her husband every year. We are not told whether they had ever taken Jesus with them before this time; they may have done so, though boys were not obliged to go up to the feasts till they were twelve years old. At that age they were supposed to enter on a new stage of their lives, as it were, and were no longer considered children. A boy was then made to begin to work regularly at his father's trade, and to commence the practice of fasting, and other religious observances.* So you see that this was what we may call a crisis in our Lord's history, and it was a very important journey that He took to Jerusalem, for He then, for the first time became, of His own Will obedient to the Ceremonial Law.

J. How far was it, Mother, from Nazareth to Jerusalem?

Mrs. H. About eighty miles, and that was a long way to go three times a year when travelling was so much more tedious than it is now. They had God's promise † that their enemies should not take advantage of the absence of

---

* Lightfoot's Works, vol. xii. p. 41.   † Exod. xxxiv. 24.

the men, to seize upon their land, but still I have often wondered how any business could have been carried on in a country where they were all called away three times a year, and most of them on long and expensive journeys. They had need of a land "flowing with milk and honey" to make up for the loss it must have caused them.

Myles. Yes, I have often thought that too. Do you think they really did go always?

Mrs. H. No, I am quite sure they did not. In Hezekiah's time, a Passover to which all the men really came, seemed quite a novelty, and most likely had not happened since the days of Solomon. I suppose that as a rule, the religious people came to the feast, and the others stayed away. But however this may have been, in our Lord's time a great multitude of people did go up to Jerusalem for the Passover. They travelled from the different towns and back again in large parties or caravans, with camels and donkeys and horses and mules. Starting from Nazareth they would probably be three days on the road, and a lovely journey they must have had. Nazareth itself

THE NOON-DAY HALT OF A CARAVAN.

is a little town situated in a hollow of the hills, which almost surround it, leaving merely an opening for the steep and narrow path by which the procession of pilgrims must have passed, in almost single file, down into the rich and fertile plain below.* This was the large plain of Jezreel which it took them the whole of their first day's march to cross.

J. Was that the same Jezreel that Elijah ran to before Ahab's chariot, just before the rain came down?

Mrs. H. Yes, it was across part of that very plain he ran. After that their road lay up and down the hills again till they reached Jerusalem. It was April then; and the beauty of the spring time in Palestine, with its brilliant sunshine, deep blue sky, and the earth carpeted with lovely flowers, cannot be imagined by those who only know our cold northern springs.

The country in Palestine, at least on this side Jordan, is exceedingly bare of trees,

---

* This is on the assumption that they did not, as some have thought, cross the Jordan, and take their journey along its eastern side, to avoid the country of the Samaritans, as was sometimes done by Galileans.

which takes off considerably from its beauty, but in a great measure this defect is compensated for, by the wonderful quantity of bright flowers which seem to come out all in a burst in the early spring. The commonest of these flowers are, I believe, anemones, and they are larger and brighter than those we have in our gardens. The scarlet ones grow quite thick on the ground like the poppies in our cornfields.

E. Mumsey, do you think Jesus ever stopped to pick the flowers?

Mrs. H. Very likely—only just then His heart must have been very full of joy and awe at the thought of the solemn feast He was about to keep for the first time. Joseph had no doubt been explaining to Him the meaning of it. You remember how in Exodus (xii. 26, 27), Moses said, "It shall come to pass when your children shall say unto you, What mean ye by this service? that ye shall say, It is the sacrifice of the Lord's Passover, Who passed over the houses of the children of Israel in Egypt, when He smote the Egyptians, and delivered our houses." I daresay the Lord Jesus had asked this very question. And again we read in Exodus xiii. 8, "And thou shalt show thy son in that day, saying, This is done because of that which the Lord did unto me when I came forth out of Egypt."

Phyllis. But didn't Jesus know all about it without any one telling Him?

Mrs. H. I should say He did not. He would have known everything, of course, if He had not chosen to clothe His Godhead with Humanity; but by doing so He shut Himself off, as it were, from His Divine Powers, putting them out of His reach. He knew what He was doing when He took upon Him our flesh, and He deliberately chose to go through with it for our sakes, though in doing so He had to humble Himself, not only by dying upon the Cross, but by living a life of "no reputation," beginning by being really and truly a Baby, just like other babies, and then a little Child, not different from* other little children, except in one thing—what was that, Elsie?

E. He was never naughty.

---

* "He had emptied Himself of His Glory: His infancy and childhood were no *mere pretence.* . . ."
  DEAN ALFORD.

Mrs. H. Exactly—He was never naughty in any way at all. He was always sweet and good. That was the only difference we should have noticed in Him.

J. Mumsey, do you think He was ever fond of playing? It isn't wrong to ask, is it?

Mrs. H. Wrong, my darling? No, of course it isn't. I should think certainly He was fond of playing when He was a little Boy; but as soon as He began to understand Who He was, and what He had been sent to the world for,* I think He must have given up His share of such childish pleasures, though I am quite sure He liked to see other children merry and happy. Happy He always was Himself—with a never-failing Source of Joy. This knowledge of His own Divinity must have been given Him by His Father in some special way, and it began probably about this time, when He was twelve years old; but His was an increasing knowledge, and perhaps was not complete, as regarded His mission here, till He was called to His public ministry, and baptized at thirty

---

* 1 John iv. 14.

years old. He lived a life of continual dependence upon His Father, and He imparted to Him according to His needs, whatever they were. But this is a very mysterious subject, and one on which it would be great presumption to speak positively.

Now tell me, Jack,—how long did the Feast of the Passover last?

J. A week.

Mrs. H. Yes, and all that time Jesus stayed at Jerusalem with His Mother and her husband.

E. Where did they sleep at night, Mumsey? Do you think they had room for them at the inn this time?

Mrs. H. I should think most likely they had, as Jerusalem was a large town, and there must have been many inns. If not, perhaps they got a room at some private house, as our Lord did afterwards when He kept His last Passover with His disciples. Or if they were unable to procure a room at all, they may have lodged outside the city wall in a tent, as many people had to do.

Ph. What did they do all the week, Mother?

Mrs. H. I can't tell you how they spent all

the time. On the first day and the last there would be a great ceremony at the Temple, called a "holy convocation," which merely means a large number of people being called together for some "holy" purpose, but exactly what the ceremony consisted of we are not told. It is quite uncertain, too, how they spent the days between; the only observances commanded by God were that every day there should be a special burnt-offering, and that no bread that had any leaven in it should be eaten during the whole of the seven days.

It was a great festival, and must have been a happy time, for then friends and relations from different parts of the country all met together, and no doubt there was a great deal of visiting and talking.

Ph. Which day was it that they had to kill and eat the Paschal lamb?

Mrs. H. They killed it on the afternoon of the first day of the feast—the 14th of the month Abib. Every household had to provide a lamb for itself, or if the family were too small to eat a whole lamb, they clubbed with a neighbour's family and had a lamb between them, which they all eat together. This must have been what Joseph and his family did.

Ph. And did they kill the lamb themselves?

Mrs. H. Yes, Joseph, as the head of his household, must have chosen a lamb, and bought it as soon as he arrived at Jerusalem, unless he had brought one with them from Nazareth, and then he must have killed it himself before the Lord's Altar, outside the Temple door, whilst the priest took the blood, which had been made to flow into a golden cup, and poured it out at the bottom of the Altar.

E. Did Joseph take Jesus with him when he went to kill the lamb?

Mrs. H. I should think so, certainly; and though this is passed over in silence, what a wonderful moment it must have been in our Lord's life! Whether it was revealed to Him that that spotless lamb was a type of Himself, and that He too must be led to the slaughter, to be sacrificed for the sins of the world, we cannot know, though we cannot help wondering. A few hours later, after sunset, the lamb was eaten at the Paschal supper. It was the 15th day of the month then, because the Jewish day began at sunset. They also eat at this supper unleavened cakes, and a sort of bitter salad, and some thick sauce, made to look like clay, to remind them of the clay of which their ancestors had to make bricks in Egypt, and into this sauce everything they eat was dipped.

E. How very nasty!

Mrs. H. It need not have been nasty, though I can't say it sounds nice. There were also three cups of red wine handed round, each of which was first blessed, and tasted by the head of the family, who was the master of the ceremonies and sat at the top of the table, and then partaken of by all the rest.

J. What do you mean, Mumsey, by the wine being "blessed"?

Mrs. H. It was called "the blessing of the wine," but I suppose it meant no more than that the master of the house gave thanks over the cup which he held in his hand, and he did so in a set form of words always used on the occasion. Between the first and second of these cups of wine going round, it was the custom for the children who were present, and if there were no children, for the youngest of the

guests, to ask—as a part of the ceremony—
"What mean ye by this service?" Then this
question was formally answered by the master
of the feast, who explained all the particulars
of the customs they observed, showing how
they were meant to commemorate the bitter
bondage of their fathers in Egypt, and their
marvellous deliverance when the Lord passed
over their houses. This explanation was called
the "showing forth,"* and it ended with a
hymn of praise.

Ph. Then I suppose when Joseph explained
all this, it was Jesus who had asked the
question?

Mrs. H. It must have been, I should think;
but as we were saying just now St. Joseph had
probably explained it all to Him before this,
and this questioning at the supper table was
merely a form.

M. Do Jews still keep the Passover in the
same way, Mother?

Mrs. H. They keep it always just before
our Easter, but very few, I think, in this

---

* To this St. Paul refers in 1 Cor. xi. 26.

country observe all these ceremonies. I don't know what they do abroad. The Paschal lamb, however, is always eaten at the Supper with the salad of herbs, and they are very particular to clear out of their houses, for that week, every particle of bread that has leaven in it.

Ph. Why was the bread they eat at the Passover to have no leaven in it?

Mrs. H. Because the Passover was a Feast holy to the Lord, and* leaven is always used in the Bible as a symbol of something bad.

E. What *is* leaven, Mumsey?

Mrs. H. It was generally a bit of old bread that was going bad, and it was mixed up in fresh bread—just a tiny little bit—to make it rise. Have you ever seen them bake bread, Elsie?

E. Oh yes, often.

Mrs. H. And haven't you noticed that it rises up at the top, and leaves the crumb part all full of little holes?

E. Yes, I know—like sponge.

Mrs. H. Exactly, and if it had no holes like

---

* Lev. ii. 11; 1 Cor. v. 6–8.

THE PASSOVER.

that, it would be hard and heavy. You know what we call "heavy" bread?

J. Yes—the bread was horridly heavy yesterday—all close and sticky. But how does putting in a bit of bad bread make it light?

Mrs. H. Anything that is decomposing, or becoming rotten and corrupt, always produces a quantity of gas, or fixed air, and this tries to rise in the dough, because it must go somewhere, and so forms a quantity of little bubbles, which make holes in the bread, without which it would be unwholesome.

Ph. I should have thought it was more unwholesome to eat all that nasty bad stuff.

Mrs. H. But you see it is such a very small quantity that is put in the bread, and the gas that it forms is not poisonous unless we breathe it in large quantities.

M. It's a filthy idea, though! Do we really have leaven in our bread?

Mrs. H. Not leaven exactly, but yeast, which is something of the same sort. The less we know about how our food is prepared, the better for our appetites, Myles, so try and forget how our bread is made! But I want you all to remember that leaven in the Bible means something corrupt and bad, though hidden out of sight. I need hardly show you how that typifies the evil so deeply seated, and often so well concealed, in the human heart. But there was One Man wholly without this evil—" Christ our Passover," who was " sacrificed for us." Think of Him sometimes to-day —that blessed, holy Child at the Paschal Feast —shrinking with all a tender-hearted child's horror from the scene of slaughter and bloodshed that He was called upon to witness for the first time, and which necessarily disfigured the purest earthly Festival; yet learning gradually, and with an interest more intense than we can realise, the deep meaning of all these wondrous types—His own beautiful and spotless Nature answering so perfectly to His Father's Mind as thus shown forth in them— and His Life day by day, and hour by hour, ascending as an Offering* of sweetest savour to rejoice His Father's Heart.

* Lev. ii. 1, 2, 11.

THE PASSOVER.

Let us pray.

Almighty God, before Whom all hearts are open, all desires known, and from Whom no secrets are hid; Cleanse the thoughts of our hearts by the inspiration of Thy Holy Spirit, that we may perfectly love Thee, and worthily magnify Thy Holy Name, through Christ our Lord. Amen.

Glory be to Jesus,
  Who in bitter pains,
Poured for me the Life-Blood
  From His sacred veins.

Grace and Life eternal
  In that Blood I find ;
Blest be His compassion,
  Infinitely kind.

Blest through endless ages
  Be the precious stream,
Which from death and ruin
  Did the world redeem.

Abel's blood for vengeance
  Pleaded to the skies ;
But the Blood of Jesus
  For our pardon cries.

Oft as earth exulting
  Wafts its praise on high,

Angel hosts rejoicing
  Make the glad reply.

Lift ye then your voices ;
  Swell the mighty flood ;
Louder still and louder
  Praise the precious Blood !

Hymns Ancient and Modern.

MODERN JERUSALEM.

CHAPTER XII.
GOD'S HOLY CHILD AT JERUSALEM.
Luke ii. 43-51.

HE next morning Myles went out fishing with his father. They had settled it the night before, and had started before any one was down. It had already become very warm, and promised to be a blazing hot day, when Mrs. Hillyard, Phyllis, Jack, and Elsie established themselves on the balcony for their Reading.

It was one of those mornings worth a special notice, as they are, alas! so rare in our short summer, which seem meant to give us an idea of what weather might be, and almost compensate for the long weary months of bitter winds and dismal wet.

The soft morning mist still lingered, and between the bright flowers on the lawn, and the hazy distance, were dotted about the scented hay-cocks in the park, whilst the river sparkled in the sunshine about half a mile off. The whole scene was transfigured by a beauty far more exquisite than that of the most perfect picture—for there was life in it—and even if you had sat with your eyes shut, the delicious, fresh, downy smell in the air—quite peculiar to that sort of day—was worth all the pictures in the stuffy rooms of the Royal Academy put together.

"What a jolly day, isn't it, Mother?" exclaimed Jack.

"Yes, very; but I have half a mind to go and sit indoors with the blinds down," answered Mrs. Hillyard.

"Go and sit indoors, Mother!" said Phyllis, "what in the world should you do that for, when it is so delicious here?"

"Why just because it is so delicious that one can do nothing but stare about. Everything looks so exquisitely beautiful this morning that I am afraid you will be hardly able to pay any attention to reading out here. Do you think you can?"

"Well, yes, I think we might if we sat with our backs to the garden, then we should have nothing to stare at but the wall of the house."

"Not a bad idea, Phyllis," answered her mother laughing. "Get your stool, Elsie, and put it down there—and, Jack, put yours the other side of the steps. Now, little people, even if you peep round, you will see nothing but leaves and roses, for the creepers are so thick you can't look through!"

"Mumsey, do let us have *one* good look round before we begin," said Phyllis. "It all looks so lovely, one feels one wants to do something more than look at it—only one doesn't quite know what!"

"One couldn't well eat it," observed Jack.

When they had laughed at this, and Mrs. Hillyard had assured Phyllis she had just the same feeling herself, only it was not easy to put it into words; they saw two figures coming across the park, one a good way ahead of the other.

"Why, there's Father and Myles!" exclaimed Jack; "do let me and Elsie run to them!"

"No, you restless child, certainly not; you

might have a sunstroke, tearing along in the hot sun without your hat. They are coming straight to us, and will be here in no time."

And in a very few minutes Myles was there, very hot and out of breath.

"I say! it *is* piping hot down there in the sun! It was no good fishing, of course, when it came out so bright: we haven't had a bite for an hour; we caught some stunning perch though before that, and the bathing was splendid."

"But, my dear boy, why did you come so fast? You look as if you were going to have a fit!"

"Oh, I daresay I do, but I shall be all right in a minute. You see I wanted to get here before you began to read. Father's coming too to-day, and I said I would run on and stop you beginning; we knew it was nearly ten o'clock—and you see I just did."

"But you read yourself, I suppose, before you went out?" asked his mother.

"Oh yes, just a little, but I wanted to come in for yours too, if I could."

"Well, dear, I can't scold you for that, but I am sorry you heated yourself so. We saw you coming, and of course we should have waited for you."

"It's all right now, Mother, anyhow—and here comes Father."

"But not quite at your pace, Myles—you ran like a lamplighter," said Mr. Hillyard, coming up the steps. "I am going to read with you to-day, Kitty, if you will have me."

"Oh, are you, James? I am so glad. We are reading in St. Luke's Gospel just now, and to-day we begin at the 43d verse of the 2nd chapter. Will you read to us as much as you think we shall get through this morning."

Mr. Hillyard then read down to the end of the 51st verse, and afterwards he said—

"First, I must ask this particularly small child a question, to see whether she has been listening. Tell me, Elsie, what happened as Joseph and Mary were coming away from Jerusalem?"

Elsie. They lost Jesus.

Mr. Hillyard. Yes, and how did they lose Him?

E. He stayed behind, and they thought He was with some of the other people, and so they never missed Him till they had travelled a whole day

Mr. H. Quite right, little one, you pay more attention than I gave you credit for! Now I mean to ask your mother a question.—Do you think, dear, that Joseph and Mary should have taken better care of the very precious Charge committed to their trust?

Mrs. Hillyard. Well, James, as a rule I do not like the plan of picking holes in the Bible saints, and settling that they were wrong here, and wrong there, when we are not told that they were, but——

Mr. H. Ah, I was sure there was a "but" coming!

Mrs. H. I am not going to say they were wrong, though—I only say perhaps they may have been a little careless—it looks rather like it. But, on the other hand, there may have been some good reason which we are not told for their thinking Jesus was quite safe with some of their friends.

Mr. H. Possibly; but I question whether the Lord would allow even a suspicion of evil to rest undeservedly on the character of any of His children, in His own Record of their conduct.

Mrs. H. You think they were careless, then?

Mr. H. I do—rather so. For a time it seems that they had forgotten Jesus. The Passover had been no doubt a busy time. They had met many old friends, and had had a great deal to talk about. Their enjoyments had not only been all very harmless, but very good; it had been what we should call a season of religious excitement. I hardly like to compare it with the great meetings that are called Conferences, Church Congresses, and Mission weeks of the present day, because it was a gathering convened directly by God, but still it had no doubt a good deal of the same social-spiritual character. This was all very delightful, or at least would have been, if it hadn't caused them to lose Jesus—but they did lose Him, because I imagine all these good things had put Him out of their minds. Do you think, Myles, that such a thing is possible now?

Myles. I can't say—I never was at any sort of great meeting in my life.

Mr. H. But, my dear fellow, I merely mean —Is it possible now to be so occupied with what people call the "things of God" as to let God Himself slip out of them unperceived? Take these Readings, for instance. We say we are occupied with Jesus very specially. Is that true? Are we so? or is it merely the things *about* Him in which we take an interest? Jack, is what I am saying all Greek to you?

Jack. Not quite, Father.

Mr. H. Phyllis, what did you think I meant?

Phyllis. I suppose you meant—do we like the Bible for God's sake—because it's about Him, and tells us how we can please Him? or do we like it because there are stories in it; or because we like finding out texts and fitting them together as we do puzzles? I can't say it better, Father.

Mr. H. You needn't, dear. You have spoken to *my* conscience, at any rate, and I think we all understood you.

Mrs. H. Let *me* give an instance, James. You know how we all enjoy our Sunday evening hymn-singing—but don't we sometimes like it so much, just for the sake of the music, that we go on quite happy, though we may have altogether ceased to be singing praise to God, and have forgotten Him?

Mr. H. I am afraid that does happen sometimes. It is a sad discovery to make—that Jesus is gone; and often it takes us much labour and sorrow to find Him again.

Ph. But you don't mean, Father, that we can be always actually thinking of God?

Mr. H. Of course not. You are not always actually thinking of me, but I may indulge the hope that if I were lost it would not be long before you found it out; and that when you speak or write to me, it is *me* that you are thinking of. But we must pass on.—When Joseph and Mary got back to Jerusalem, where did they find Jesus?

E. In the Temple, sitting with the doctors.

Mr. H. Yes, "both hearing them, and asking them questions." But you know, Elsie, these men were not what *we* call doctors, as St. Luke was; they were teachers of the law, and had a kind of school in a part of the Temple building, where they gave public instruction. What do you think Jesus was doing there, Myles?

M. He was learning about the law, wasn't He?

Mr. H. Yes, the doctors were teaching Him, "and all that heard Him were astonished at

His understanding and answers." They had never had such a pupil before!

Ph. Father, there is a picture in our big Bible of "Christ disputing with the Doctors." What does that mean?

Mr. H. It means arguing with them, and setting them right. Some people have thought that our Lord went there to *teach* them, instead of to *learn* from them. Tell us what you think about it, Kitty.

Mrs. H. I cannot think it would have been like Jesus, Who was perfect in all His ways, to stand teaching a set of learned old men when He was only twelve years old. He could be no Example for children if that had been His work, for certainly it is their place to learn and not to teach. I dislike that picture very much, and the declamatory, unchildlike attitude in which He is made to stand. There is another very beautiful * picture, though, that I have seen on the same subject, but even that gives a wrong idea, for He was *sitting* we are expressly told, and sitting no doubt at the feet † of His teachers.

---

* By Mr. Holman Hunt.   † See Acts xxii. 3.

Mr. H. Certainly; but I think the last picture you refer to most likely represents the moment after He had risen from His seat, and His Mother is drawing Him away. If so, the idea is a true one. But I perfectly agree with you that He was there to learn, although in doing so He has taught a lesson of humility to all generations. I believe myself that He was taught like other children through human teachers. He learnt to read* and write † at Nazareth, but at Jerusalem He had opportunities of instruction in the written law of God, such as probably He never before enjoyed, and you see, Myles, with what diligence He availed Himself of them. No doubt, like David, He "rejoiced at God's Word like one that findeth great spoil," and "had more understanding than all His teachers," and yet with His meek and teachable spirit that did not prevent Him from learning thankfully whatever they could teach Him.

M. But wouldn't those Rabbis have taught their pupils lots of rubbish? I thought they believed all kinds of bosh themselves.

---

* Luke iv. 16. † John viii. 6.

Mr. H. So they did, a good deal, at least, though there were one or two really good men amongst them at that time—but their foolish additions to the truth would fall off harmless from a Mind that could not be injured by them; for Jesus was in continual dependence on a Higher Teaching than theirs, and He received the Law from their lips, "not as the word of men, but as it is in truth, the Word of God." The Scribes and Pharisees still "sat in Moses' seat,"* as Christ many years afterwards reminded the Jewish people; and as the authorised teachers, He paid them the respect due to their office.

J. One can't fancy Jesus doing lessons, can one, Mother?

Mrs. H. It seems very wonderful, and yet He was always learning throughout His life on earth. There is a beautiful passage in Isaiah—find it, children, and I will read it to you. It is in the 50th chapter and 4th verse. Remember it is Jesus speaking—"The Lord God hath given Me the tongue of the learned, that I

---

* Matt. xxiii. 2, 3.

should know how to speak a word in season to him that is weary: He wakeneth morning by morning, He wakeneth mine ear to hear with the attention of a learner."* It was thus, because He was such an attentive Learner, that He was such a Great Teacher, when the right time came—and always knew how to speak— how to comfort, and cheer, and rebuke, and exhort. As He heard, He spoke.†

E. Were His parents angry with Him at all, do you think, Mumsey, that He had remained behind?

Mrs. H. They were "exceedingly ‡ amazed" at finding Him there, all alone, and not afraid of all these learned men, but "asking them questions." It seems, if one may venture to say so, as though He was so bent on learning all He could, and was so entranced with interest in the "wondrous things" of God's law, that He lost all sense of shyness, or of the flight of time. I think there is a shade of annoyance in His Mother's remonstrance, and that was natural, as she could not fully understand the Mind of her

---
* Bishop Lowth's translation.   † John v. 30; xv. 15.
‡ Literal translation.

Son, nor the powerful attraction His Father's Words must have had for Him. She speaks as a fond and anxious mother would do—" Son, why hast Thou thus dealt with us? behold, Thy father and I have sought Thee sorrowing."

Mr. H. " Sorrowing " is perhaps a hardly strong enough word either for their grief at losing Him. It is the same word in the original as that translated "torments," and "tormented," in Luke xvi. 23, 24, where the rich man in our Lord's parable describes his feelings when "in hell." *

Ph. How miserable they must have been then! They were punished for losing Jesus, weren't they?—if it was their fault.

Mrs. H. Indeed they were!—But as we have noticed where the Blessed Virgin was probably wrong, do let me call every one's attention to the beautiful unselfish way in which she puts Joseph first—mentioning *his* sorrow before her own, and so simply and naturally, with her own lovely humility, taking the second place, even when speaking to Him who was her own Son, but Joseph's only by adoption.

---

* This similarity of expression has been noticed by Dr. Goulburn in his "Gospel of the Childhood."

Mr. H. Yes, I never observed that—it is beautiful,—especially as we see from the very fact that *she* was the speaker, that she did not hesitate to exercise her own peculiar authority with her Son. There was a Divine sublimity in His answer, however, that she was not prepared for. She had spoken of Joseph as His "father," and no doubt till then Jesus had been in the habit of calling him so; but now He lays claim, perhaps for the first time, to a Relationship to which He owes His first allegiance—" How is it that ye sought me? Wist ye not that I must be about My FATHER'S business?"*

These are the only words He ever really spoke as a Child that have been handed down to us—but how we at once recognise His Voice, even in this short sentence! He speaks here as He always spoke afterwards, and as "never man spake"—simply, and even humbly, but with the Majesty of the Godhead in His tone.

M. It seems very strange they didn't understand Him, particularly as each of them had

---

* Or "In My Father's precincts."

been distinctly told that Jesus was to be the Son of God.

Mr. H. It does—"But His Mother kept all these sayings in her heart," until the day came when the full force of them was made known to her.

M. When was that, Father?

Mr. H. I think it was not till the Day of Pentecost* that she understood them quite. The "Comforter" then brought to her remembrance, as to the Apostles', "all things"† that Jesus had said, and taught them to understand them too. And it was she, we may feel sure, who gave to St. Luke all such particulars of our Lord's Infancy and Childhood as are to be found in his Gospel. She must have lived with the disciples, and he could hardly have failed to ask her, first of all, everything he wished to know on these subjects; he tells us that he derived his information from eye-witnesses, and of course she was one of them. In the meantime her Son returned to Nazareth, and she and Joseph found that the Heavenly "Business" upon which He was

---

* See Acts i. 14, and ii. 1, 2.   † John xiv. 26.

entering with a renewed consecration, was not one which would interfere with their claims, for it took in Joseph's "business" too. What was that, Jack?

J. Carpentering.

Mr. H. Yes—the work which God gave His Son to do as a Child was to learn. To learn the letter of the law from the Rabbis when He was at Jerusalem; to learn carpentering from Joseph in His quiet home at Nazareth; to learn directly from that "book of the law" which never departed from His mouth, and in which He meditated* day and night; and to learn obedience continually "by the things which He suffered." †

Mrs. H. It is time to stop now, James, but do come and talk a little more with us about Christ's Nazareth life to-morrow.

Mr. H. Very well. There is a beautiful description of the place in this book here, which I will read to you then, and I am sure you will all like to hear it, *though* it was written by a schoolmaster. ‡

---

* Josh. i. 8. † Heb. v. 8.
‡ Dr. Farrar—then of Marlborough College.

O

J. Oh my!

Mr. H. It is not the least dry, I assure you, and was written, I believe, on the spot. He went to Palestine on purpose to write the book.

J. Thanks, Father! I should really like to hear it—awfully. Can't you read it now?

Mr. H. No, not now, it is getting late, and you will have quite as much as you can do this morning to get your lessons done in time to go to the cricket-match.

Mrs. H. Besides, dear, I want you to carry away on your mind to-day—that restless little mind of yours, that won't keep many thoughts in it at one time!—not a picture of Nazareth, so much as of Him for Whose Sake that place is dear to us. Try and think of Him a little to-day, and of how diligent He was to learn—and do your lessons well for His Sake.

Mr. Hillyard closed the Reading with this prayer—

O Almighty God, Whom truly to know is everlasting life; Grant us perfectly to know Thy Son Jesus Christ to be the Way, the Truth, and the Life; that following

GOD'S HOLY CHILD.

in His steps, we may steadfastly walk in the way that leadeth to Eternal Life; through the same Thy Son Jesus Christ our Lord. Amen.

MY God, my life, my love,
To Thee, to Thee, I call;
I cannot live if Thou remove,
For Thou art all in all.

To Thee and Thee alone,
The angels owe their bliss;
They stand around Thy gracious Throne,
And dwell where Jesus is.

Not all the harps above,
Can make a heavenly place;
If God His residence remove,
Or but conceal His Face.

Nor earth, nor all the sky,
Can one delight afford,
No not a drop of real joy
Without Thy Presence, Lord.
—WATTS.

LORD, if Thou Thy Grace impart,
Poor in spirit, meek in heart,
I shall as my Master be
Clothèd with humility.

Simple, teachable, and mild,
Changed into a little child,
Pleased with all the Lord provides,
Weaned from all the world besides.

Father, fix my soul on Thee ;
Every evil let me flee ;
Nothing want beneath, above,
Happy in Thy precious Love.

O that all may seek and find
Every good in Christ combined ;
Him let Israel still adore,
Trust Him, praise Him evermore !
—CHARLES WESLEY.

CHAPTER XIII.
GOD'S HOLY CHILD AT NAZARETH.

LUKE II. 51 (*first clause*).

"HERE I am," said Mr. Hillyard next morning, as he came into his wife's sitting-room with a thick book under his arm, "but where are the children? They were calling under my window that it was past the time, and now there isn't one of them to be seen."

"Not seen, but *heard*, I think," answered Mrs Hillyard. "Listen!"

"What on earth are they about, making all that din?"

"I think the bees must be swarming!" explained his wife. "Williams always celebrates that occasion by drumming on a tin tray with a shovel."

"Then I am to understand that everything is at a stand-still until the bees have swarmed?"

"Perhaps you had better go down to the kitchen garden—that is where the noise seems to come from—and see yourself what is going on. All I know is, that without a moment's warning the family rushed out of the window, and ran shouting down the garden. They had no time for explanations."

Mr. Hillyard took his wife's advice, and proceeded to the kitchen garden. It was not for a considerable time, however, that he re-appeared, in charge of his four children.

"I hope the event has gone off to every one's satisfaction," observed Mrs. Hillyard, "especially to the bees', but I really began to despair of our reading this morning."

"We are so sorry!" exclaimed all the party.

"We weren't any of us stung, though, Mumsey," said Elsie, "and the bees did look so funny!"

"Come now! the sooner we begin the better," said their father; "I shall be happy to take the chair at this meeting, if Jack will put it outside for me. I conclude we need not be boxed up here this lovely morning."

So—as before—they settled themselves on the balcony, and Mr. Hillyard, producing his large book, commenced reading the description of Nazareth, and the daily life of the peasants there, at the present day, which is to be found at the end of this volume. It is not put in here, as it would make this chapter too long, but any one can read it that likes. When he stopped Elsie said,

"Go on, Father, don't shut the book—you are just getting to the nice part now."

"And pray what do you call the 'nice part'?"

"Why, I want to hear some stories about Jesus when He was little. Mother said there were none in the Bible, but I thought you were going to read us some out of this other book."

"But there is nothing really true about Jesus told anywhere except in the Bible, so you must be satisfied with that. There were spurious (that means sham) Gospels written long ago, when such cheating couldn't be found out as quickly as it would be now, some of them very soon after St. John died, and one of these * tells plenty of stories about the childhood of 'Jesus,' but they are utter rubbish, and very profane besides."

"What sort of stories, Father?" asked Jack; "do tell us."

"They are stories very much of the same sort as fairy stories. I remember one was about some women who were found feeding, and kissing, and crying over a mule, who had a smart silk shawl on, and an ebony collar round his neck, and who do you think he was?"

"Oh, their husband or brother, of course," answered Jack.

"I was sure you would know, being up in the 'Arabian Nights'! Yes, he was their brother, but had had the misfortune to be bewitched by some female admirers who were jealous of him, and so had been a mule for years."

"And then he came right again?" inquired little Elsie.

"Yes, then of course he came right again,

---

* The Gospel of the Infancy.

but you must excuse me telling you how, for that part of the story I should be sorry to repeat."

"Father, please tell us another!" pleaded Jack and Elsie.

"Very well, I will tell you just one more, and I am sure you will think that sufficient —at any rate you ought. Joseph, it seems from what this 'Gospel' tells us, was not much of a carpenter, and yet the 'King of Jerusalem,' whoever that may have been, sent for him to make him a throne. Whether the throne was so very grand, or Joseph was so very clumsy, I can't tell you, but it took him two whole years to make, and when it was finished it was four 'spans' too short for the space it was to occupy. Upon this discovery the king was in a great rage, and poor Joseph, whether from fright or sulks we are not told, went supperless to bed. The next day—the story says—'Jesus' told him not to distress himself the least about his bad work, it would come all right and square if they only pulled it. So each of them took a side and pulled, and lo and behold! it just fitted into its place. 'Jesus' had worked a miracle to rectify Joseph's blunders, and to reward him, apparently, for his abominable carelessness."

"A nice moral, certainly," observed Mrs. Hillyard.

"Very—what you may call thoroughly practical teaching," said her husband smiling.

"It would be jolly for us, Myles, wouldn't it?" asked Jack, "if we could get our lessons done for us by a miracle that way, and all our bad sums made right!"

"Hush, Jack!—I think these idiotic stories are of immense value in one way," continued Mr. Hillyard, "for how they set off the Bible! —showing us what was the standard of morality prevalent at that time, and how low man must have sunk to have such ideas of the Divine; and therefore of course how impossible it was that such a book as the Bible could have been written except by direct inspiration. Whenever men attempted of themselves to write a life of Christ, this is the sort of thing they produced. All the miracles in the Apocryphal books are of the same senseless sort, except when they were evidently taken from the true

Gospel history; and I particularly want you children to notice this—it is so very important —that never in the Bible are what we may call *fairy-story miracles* worked. No poor people ever come across treasures of gold, no idle beggars ever become princes. Those who by some special misfortune had fallen out of the ranks, are started fair again with the rest of their hard-working, suffering fellow-creatures, but that is all. There is never a waste of power, and no sentimental overdoing of kindness."

"Exactly so," said Mrs. Hillyard. "But now we must read once more the first part of the 51st verse of the 2nd chapter of St. Luke. We shall not get through more than that, I am sure, to-day.—'And He went down with them, and came to Nazareth, and was subject unto them.' —Jack, what does 'subject' mean?"

"Obedient, doesn't it?"

"Yes, it means that Jesus was placed beneath His parents, and took a real child's place, as we said yesterday; and not only as a Child, but to the very end of His earthly Life, He was 'subject.' He always 'submitted Himself to every ordinance of man for the Lord's sake,' * as you will find in the course of the Gospel history."

"That is very true, dear," said Mr. Hillyard, "and let me observe that from the time of His return to Nazareth, after His first Passover, He probably began His life of toil as a carpenter's apprentice. Now how may we suppose He did His work? Eh, Myles?"

"Why well, of course," said Myles.

"You don't think if *He* had had a cupboard to make it would have been too short for its place?"

"No," said Myles smiling.

"You think His work was done well to order, and turned out true and square?"

"Of course."

"And sent punctually to the customer, and fairly charged for?"

"James," whispered Mrs. Hillyard, "don't you think you are going a little too far?"

"Not unless Jesus went too far, dear. Don't let us be kept back by any superstitious fear of irreverence, from gazing steadily at the Example

---

* 1 Peter ii. 13.

He set us. No, my boys, remember that He did His work like a man, and would have been ashamed to have made a bad job of any part of it, or to have slurred over a difficulty. Every bit of His work would have borne inspection— though He was often hot and tired. God grant you may remember that, and go and do your own work faithfully, 'knowing that you have a Master in Heaven' Who once earned His daily bread, not helped out by miracles, but by the sweat of His brow."

"Somehow one can't realise it, can one?" said Myles. " Fancy the other boys treating Him like one of themselves! Jesus was quite a common name, wasn't it?"

"Yes, quite, as common as John or Thomas is with us. That sacred ' Name which is above every name' was shouted by His playmates on the hill-side of Nazareth, amid peals of merry laughter, and called out continually in Joseph's workshop when Jesus was sent on an errand. It is no real love that we have for Him, if these considerations make it less sacred to us now. But He was a very different Hero from Homer's, wasn't He, Myles?"

"Yes, I was just thinking so."

"And from all the demi-gods of the heathen—and yet every one of these mythologies teaches us how truly the God Incarnate was the 'Desire of all nations.'"

"And yet only He could meet the real needs of His fellow-workers and fellow-sufferers," said Mrs. Hillyard.

"Yes, of young and old, and rich and poor; and He does meet them exactly," answered her husband.

"I was telling the children the other day," said Mrs Hillyard, "that Jesus was always happy—do you think I was right?"

"'Sorrowful, yet always rejoicing,' I should say—but that is easier said than understood. It means, I think, that there is a Joy so deep-seated that no troubles can shake it—and yet they are felt—possibly more deeply than when happiness is on the surface. Our Lord must have suffered much even as a Child."

"No doubt," said Mrs Hillyard. "He loved His Mother, as no other son ever loved a mother in this cold world, and He loved Joseph too, and He was 'subject unto them;' and He loved

His brothers and sisters and friends; and yet they were all sinners, and their sins were as hateful to Him as they themselves were dear. His keen* sense of right gave Him just as keen a sense of wrong. He loathed evil and yet He was surrounded by it. With His sensitiveness to sin, He must have felt His Mother's faults in every fibre of His Pure and Holy Being, and yet never once did He fail in respect, or affection, or obedience to her.—Think of that, dear children, next time I am unkind, or unjust to you; or when you notice some nasty little fault in me that irritates you."

"My dear, I don't see that you need run yourself down," remarked Mr. Hillyard.

"Mumsey, it's horrid of you to talk like that!" exclaimed Phyllis, "you know you are the greatest darling . . . ."

Myles, Jack, and Elsie seconded this amendment rather noisily.

"Now, hush, all of you! Don't say I am never tiresome, because you all know quite well I am.—Indeed, it seems almost wrong to

---

* Isa. xi. 3. (marg.)

appear to compare myself for a moment with St. Mary. But still it may help you to form a faint idea of what it must have been for Jesus! Just try and think of it if you can. For however sweet and holy His Mother was, she was still a sinner—and she often misunderstood Him too, whilst His neighbours, and even His own brothers,* disbelieved in Him all the time He lived with them."

"That must have been dreadfully trying for Him!" exclaimed Phyllis.

"Indeed it must—and besides those troubles which were, in their degree at least, peculiar to Himself, He had, I cannot doubt, His share of common little childish troubles, such as you have yourselves. It is well to put this forward, because we want children to understand that there is no trouble that they can have that they need be afraid to take straight to Jesus, and to tell Him all about; feeling quite sure that He will enter into it much better than any one else can, and will feel for every little child with all His Heart. Elsie, do you know what 'sympathy' means?"

---

* John vii. 5.

"No, Mother."

"Can you tell her, Jack?"

"It means somebody being sorry for you when you are unhappy."

"It means more than that—it means somebody feeling your trouble *with* you. You see the difference?—and you have felt the difference. Tell me, Elsie, when you are very unhappy about anything, to whom would you rather go to be comforted,—to a grown-up person or a child?"

"To a grown-up person, I think, Mumsey."

"No doubt you would, though you couldn't perhaps say why. I think the reason is because grown-up people are not so thoughtless, and they have had so much more trouble themselves, that they know better what to say. But still they are often poor comforters, particularly to children, however kind they may be, because they have bad memories, and things that happened long ago seem dim and unreal, so that they can't remember exactly how they felt themselves when *they* were children. All that they have gone through since has made their own childish sorrows seem small, and therefore

P

their children's seem small too. But it is never like that with Jesus. His memory is always fresh, and His own little troubles at Nazareth are as present to His Mind as though they were happening at this minute, so that whilst He has all a child's understanding of what you feel, He has more than even a mother's sympathy—and nothing seems little to Him."

"And then," added Phyllis, "He can really help us to bear things."

"Yes, dear child, I am glad you have found that out; and I do trust you may all make a Friend of Him in that way—asking Him for things you really want, and not saying fine things to Him because you think you ought."

"Thank you, Kitty," said Mr. Hillyard, "I don't mind saying that I would far rather hear my children praying that a lost dog might be found, than for a hundred spiritual blessings they didn't feel their need of. To believe that 'God Is,' and to be *true* with Him, is the main thing."

"Father," said Elsie, "that is the very thing I did ask Jesus for the other day, when Snip was lost, and he walked in almost directly after."

"Yes, little one, I said it on purpose, because I hoped some of you had prayed for that—I knew you were very unhappy about it. Only remember, Elsie, people don't always get their prayers answered like that ; we often ask God for things that He knows we should be much better without. So if Snip had not come back, it would not have been because God took no notice of your prayer.

"But there was one very great sorrow our Blessed Lord and His Mother had to bear whilst they lived in Galilee. Who knows what that was?"

As none of the children answered, Mrs. Hillyard asked,

" Do you mean Joseph's death?"

"Yes, I do. We are not told anything about it, but the after history, according to all the Evangelists, plainly shows that he was dead before Christ's Ministry began. We know very little about him, yet from that little we can feel sure that he was one whom Jesus must have dearly loved. We know that he was 'a just man,' and his great kindness, and wonderful faith in God prove him to have been no common character.

From the time of Joseph's death until Christ's public Work began, He most likely supported His mother Himself,* by His own labour as a Carpenter; patiently working and waiting till His Father's time came to call Him to another, but not a higher sphere of labour. Whatever is God's Will must be the very best and highest service for any one, whether we speak of our Master, or of ourselves.—But I must leave you now, when we have said a few words in prayer; and if I were you, Kitty, I would continue this subject next time."

"We will," answered Mrs. Hillyard, "and I hope you will come and tell us more about it; I am sure we have not thought enough of Christ's Life at Nazareth."

"I doubt if I ever thought of it at all," said Myles.

"Well then, dear, ask God not to let you forget it now."

And so the Reading ended for that morning.

---

* See Mark vi. 3.

GOD'S HOLY CHILD.

Almighty God, Who hast given Thine only Son to be unto us both a Sacrifice for sin, and also an Ensample of godly life; Give us grace that we may always most thankfully receive that, His inestimable benefit, and also daily endeavour to follow the blessed steps of His most holy life; through the same Jesus Christ our Lord. Amen.

(Collect for 2nd Sunday after Easter.)

In a carpenter's poor cottage
   Thirty years our Saviour dwelt,
Subject to His earthly parents,
   On His Father's work intent.

But that work, dear little children,
   Was to suffer and be still,
Though around Him Satan triumphed,
   Leading captives at his will.

Sure the holy Heart of Jesus
   Felt the sorrow and the shame,
Deeply felt the foul dishonour
   Done unto His Father's Name.

Felt the power was strong within Him,
   Sin to conquer, God to own,
But the evil He reprovèd
   By His holy life alone.

Though He came to preach the Gospel,
  Though He came the sick to heal,
Though He came to cast out devils,
  And His Father to reveal :

Yet till God the Father called Him,
  Quietly His course He ran,
Winning by His life most holy,
  Favour sweet from God and man.

Learn by this, O Christian children,
  What the Lord would have you do,
How you best may render service,
  Loving, hearty, faithful, true.

Learn—for till your life be holy,
  And your lamp doth brightly shine,
No true witness can you render
  To the law of Love divine.

And be sure that living witness
  Glory for our God will gain,
And by this His Benediction
  His dear Children will obtain.
    Verses for the Seasons of the Christian Year.

COME, sing with holy gladness,
  High Alleluias sing,
Uplift your loud Hosannas
  To Jesus, Lord and King ;
For Jesus is salvation,
  And glory, grace, and rest :
To babe, and boy, and maiden
  The one Redeemer Blest.

O boys, be strong in Jesus,
　To toil for Him is gain ;
And Jesus wrought with Joseph
　With chisel, saw, and plane.
O maidens, live for Jesus,
　Who was a maiden's Son ;
Be patient, pure, and gentle,
　And perfect grace begun.

Soon in the Golden City
　The boys and girls shall play,
And through the dazzling mansions
　Rejoice in endless day ;
For Christ will bring His children,
　With that triumphant throng,
Through the bright pearly portals,
　To sing the eternal song.
　　　　　　Hymns Ancient and Modern.

CHAPTER XIV.
GROWTH.

Luke ii. 52.

THE bright sunshine was all gone next day. There had been a thunderstorm in the night, and it was cold and wet. The children were glad enough to turn away from the window, for outside everything was dripping and cheerless. Jack and Elsie declared they liked a wet day immensely; but Mr. Hillyard was probably of a different opinion— he had been obliged to go up to London, and was now enjoying a long drive to the station.

"I am so sorry your father will not be with us to-day," said Mrs. Hillyard, "but we must try and do the best we can without him. You remember he said that we had better continue the subject of Christ's Life at Nazareth, so our portion this morning will be merely these words—'And Jesus increased in wisdom, as in age, and in favour with God and man.'—That is perhaps the best translation of the verse, and whilst it does not limit His growth to His mere height, yet of course the word 'age' includes that. Have any of you any questions to ask?"

Jack. I have, Mother. If we are to read at *this* rate, I want to know how long we may expect to be getting through one of the Gospels —let alone four?

Mrs. Hillyard. That is a calculation I have no time to make, my son; but please remember that just now the early part of the History of Christ's Life is much more important for all of you to think about, than the latter, and therefore we are dwelling much more upon it. Perhaps we may read a chapter or two at a time presently.

J. But why, Mumsey?

Mrs. H. Because Christ *as a Child* is your Example now. Indeed He is more of an Example to all of us during these unrecorded years, than afterwards. During His public Ministry, He was engaged in a Work which was peculiarly His own, and to which none of us could possibly be called.

Myles. But, Mother, if He was to be more particularly our Example in His Youth, why aren't we told more about Him then?

Phyllis. Yes, it does seem very strange that when Luke could have asked Mary all about that time at Nazareth, he didn't tell us more about it. Of course he must have known ever so much more than He wrote, and he might have told so many stories about Jesus when He was a Child, and a Boy, and a young Man.

Elsie. Mumsey, don't you wish he had?—I do so much!

Mrs. H. It would be most extraordinary, certainly, that he should have said so little, if the Bible had been like any other book, but then, you see, it isn't. Remember that God wrote it, and He would never say anything unnecessary. He didn't think it right to gratify our curiosity about things that it would be better for us not to know.

M. I am sure you are right, Mother—only I don't see it. I can't help thinking that it would have been a great help to us to know more about Christ's early Life, for how can we copy Him at that time when we know next to nothing as to how He behaved, or what He said and did?

Mrs. H. We know that He lived quietly at home with Joseph and Mary, and " was subject unto them . . . and increased in wisdom . . . and in favour with God and man."

M. Yes, but that is so vague.

Mrs. H. It is concise, but I do not think vague. Yesterday, when we considered His subjection to His parents, we found how very much was contained in a few of those words. We saw that they included study, and obedience, and submission, and manual labour; and the incident in the Temple at Jerusalem proved that His earthly duties were performed for His Heavenly Father. It is not as if we didn't know the principles and rules of conduct that guided Him. We know quite well what they were from the rest of the Bible, and specially from His own teaching afterwards—such as the Sermon on the Mount. He walked by the same Rule all through His Life, whatever His

Work was, and that Rule was the very same which we have ourselves—the Word of God; and It is enough for us.

M. You think particular instances of His conduct in His daily Life would have been no good to us then?

Mrs. H. I am sure we are better without them. If instances had been given, they would probably never have corresponded exactly with our own circumstances, and all kinds of follies would have been practised by well-intentioned people, wishing to imitate Him in the letter, though they could not in the spirit—at least it appears so to me. Besides, it might have given rise to a good deal of irreverence. There are very irreverent speculations made even as it is, by people who have theories to support about His Human Nature; and it would have been much worse if they had had more texts to argue from on subjects they cannot possibly understand.

Ph. One thing, Mother, I should immensely like to know—what He was like to look at. Did nobody ever say?

Mrs. H. Nobody. The only account on

record of His Personal Appearance is evidently a forgery.

Ph. Shouldn't you very much like to know, Myles?

M. Yes, I should. But as you say, Mother, no doubt it is better we shouldn't.

Mrs. H. I think it is very clearly better that we shouldn't, for many reasons. But it is a wonderful thought that though we may not know it, He *had* a certain definite Appearance with all Its own individual peculiarities of Face and Figure ; and a certain type of features, and colouring, and temperament. Of course one can't help wondering what that was.

E. How I wish we could have seen Him!

Mrs. H. It is a very natural wish, darling— like the hymn you say sometimes—

"I think, when I read that sweet Story of old,
    When Jesus was here among men,
How He called little children as lambs to His fold,
    I should like to have been with Him then.

"I wish that His hand had been laid on my head,
    That His arms had been thrown around me,
And that I might have seen His kind look when He said,
    'Let the little ones come unto Me.'"

But though it is such a natural wish, I think it is a mistaken one, and that it would have been no real spiritual advantage to us to have known " Christ after the flesh."*

Ph. Don't you really, Mother?

Mrs. H. I do not indeed. As to its making it any easier to us to believe in Him, it strikes me it would have been a great deal more difficult. To believe that a certain young Carpenter with Whom we were acquainted, and Whom we had perhaps ourselves employed, and Whose family were all well known amongst us as respectable working people—was the Son of God!—must have required a larger measure of faith, I think, than is needed by us who have always been accustomed to idealise both Him and them.

Ph. Well perhaps it would—I see what you mean.

Mrs. H. Soon we shall see that this was just the difficulty that His neighbours at Nazareth † had to contend with, when for the first time He appeared amongst them as a Teacher. " Is not this the Carpenter!" they said—"the son

---

* 2 Cor. v. 16.   † Luke iv. 16–22.

of Mary, the brother of James, and Joses, and of Judah and Simon? and are not His sisters here with us? And they were offended at Him."* Still let us not forget that in either case true faith is the gift of God, for only God † can so reveal Him to us as really to profit us.

But we must consider our verse a little more closely.—We are told that Jesus grew, bodily and spiritually;—I think it is not an irreverent inquiry—How did He grow? were there any means employed in His growth, as in our own, or was it a miraculous growth, independent of all means?—But the little ones won't understand this. Do you know, Elsie, what makes you grow?

E. Nothing *makes* me, Mumsey; children always grow.

Mrs. H. You would not grow without nourishment, little one, any more than the flowers in your garden would grow if they were never watered. Some poor little children who don't get half enough to eat, hardly grow at all,

---

* Mark vi. 3.   † Matt. xvi. 16, 17.

and are miserable stunted little things. It is your food, and your sleep at night, and the fresh air you breathe that make you grow, because they keep you well and strong. Your food actually becomes part of your body, for it makes your blood, and muscles, and bones. You are always wearing them out, and your food is always making them again.

E. Is it? how funny!

Mrs. H. Yes, and we have no reason whatever to suppose that it was otherwise with Jesus. If He was really and truly a Human Being, as we are told He was, His bodily growth must have depended, like yours, on food and sleep. But the soul wants food too, if it is to grow, and St. Luke tells us that Christ also "increased in Wisdom, and in favour with God and man." May we suppose that that growth, too, in His case, depended upon means?

M. I know you think it did, Mother, but I don't know what.

Mrs. H. Perhaps we may be able again to judge from our own experience, Christ being indeed our Brother. If we are growing in Wisdom, and in likeness to Him, what is the

GROWTH.

spiritual food that produces that growth in us?

M. Oh, I see now what you mean—the Bible.

Mrs. H. Yes, the Bible. That is to say the truth about God that is in the Bible: for some Christians can't read, or they may have lived where they couldn't get a Bible, but some of the Truth that is in it reached them, and on that they fed and grew.

Ph. Mother, I thought you were going to say Prayer.

Mrs. H. So I was, too. We must not separate prayer from the study of the Bible, for the Holy Scriptures would do us no good without prayer, neither could we pray according to God's Will without some knowledge of the Scriptures. The two things must go together, as they did in the case of our Blessed Lord. His direct Communion with His Father was the means of growth and sustenance to Him, but His Prayers were ever in perfect harmony with the Written Word, which was His constant study. Do you understand me?

Ph. Oh yes, I do quite now.

Mrs. M. And do let us all remember that it

Q

is a very great responsibility to have a Bible, and to be able to read it. It contains the living and life-giving Word of God, which alone can give spiritual Life to our souls in the first place, or can keep It growing when It is given. Myles, will you read James i. 18, as far as the first comma.

M. "Of His own Will begat He us with the Word of Truth."

Mrs. H. Now, Phyllis, please read 1 Peter i. 23.

Ph. "Being born again, not of corruptible seed, but of incorruptible, by the Word of God, which liveth and abideth for ever."

Mrs. H. These verses mean that the great Change in us, when we first really take Jesus as our own Saviour, is brought about by our believing the "report"* of Him in the Bible, so that through It we are said to be "born." Now, Jack, you read 1 Peter ii. 2.

J. "As new-born babes, desire the sincere milk of the Word, that ye may grow thereby."

Mrs. H. Yes—"that ye may grow thereby."

---

* Isa. liii. 1 ; 1 John v. 9–12.

That proves the other point, you see, that by means of God's Word we are not only "born," but we also "grow."

M. That is what Christ said to the devil, isn't it? or something very like it. At His temptation, I mean.

Mrs. H. You mean "Man shall not live by bread alone, but by every Word that proceedeth from the mouth of God"?

M. Yes.

Mrs. H. Precisely so: and His example then, as well as what He said, enforced the same truth; for each answer that He made to the enemy was a Scripture quotation. The one you have alluded to is from Deuteronomy (chap. viii. 3). And though our Blessed Lord required no new birth, yet doubtless it was thus—through the nourishment of the living Word of God—that He *grew* in wisdom, and in favour with God and man. His delight in learning from the book of the law in the Temple, and the deep knowledge He showed of it in His Teaching later on, prove how He had been rooted and grounded in that Source of Heavenly Wisdom. And thus, in His diligent study of His Father's Word, He is very specially our Example.

M. Mother, isn't it said of some one in the Old Testament that he "grew in favour with God and man?"

Mrs. H. Yes, it is said of Samuel—here it is—in 1 Sam. ii. 26. "And the child Samuel grew on, and was in favour both with the Lord, and also with men." And we may notice that the Word was even in Old Testament times the principle of Life and Growth. See what David said about it in Ps. cxix. 93.

M. "I will never forget Thy precepts: for with them Thou hast quickened me."

Mrs. H. "Quickened" is an old-fashioned word, meaning *made alive.*

Ph. Like "the quick and the dead" in the Creed, isn't it, Mother? Doesn't that mean the living and the dead?

Mrs. H. Yes, dear, I am glad you remembered it. Now look for Prov. iii. 1–4.

Ph. "My son, forget not My law; but let thine heart keep My commandments. For length of days, and long life, and peace shall they add unto thee. Let not mercy and truth

forsake thee; bind them about thy neck;*
write them upon the table of thy heart : † So
shalt thou find favour and good understanding
in the sight of God and man."

M. What a splendid commentary that makes
on our verse, doesn't it, Mother?

Mrs H. Indeed it does. St. Luke quoted it,
no doubt, thus showing that he had in his
mind — or rather may we not say that the
Holy Ghost had in *His* Mind?—that one ‡
"spiritual meat" by which the whole family
of God are ever fed. But have any of you
any other question to ask before we close?

M. I should like to know about Jesus growing in favour with *man.* He didn't seem in
favour with people generally, afterwards. He
couldn't have been, or they wouldn't have killed
Him.

Mrs. H. No, but that was after He became
a public Teacher, and exhorted, and rebuked,
and threatened them. Then they hated Him;
He was a hindrance to them, and they wished
to get Him out of the way. His Sinlessness

---

* Deut vi. 6–9.   † Jer. xxxi. 33; 2 Cor. iii. 3.   ‡ 1 Cor. x. 3.

only exasperated them, because they wanted to find an accusation against Him and could not. And yet even then they were forced to admire Him. They "wondered at the gracious words that proceeded out of His mouth," and declared that "never man spake like this Man." But when He was a Boy, His Goodness did not interfere with the grown-up people about Him— quite the contrary; they liked Him the better for it, for they found He was always unselfish, and kind, and willing, and obliging. I daresay many a neighbour, worried with tiresome, disobedient, quarrelsome children of her own, had said to Mary—" How I envy you that Boy of yours—He is so good and so trustworthy— what a comfort He must be to you!"

J. Perhaps the other children didn't like Him so much.

Mrs. H. I daresay not, for He would be more or less a reproach to them. He could never have joined them in anything wrong, and the naughty ones must have felt His company burdensome. That must have been a great sorrow to Him, for many little things we are told about Him show that He was sociable and friendly, and so to be shunned and disliked by any of His companions when He would so gladly have made them all happy, must have been a peculiar trial, and one which, I think, Myles, you can in a measure understand.

M. Why *me* particularly, Mother?

Mrs. H. Because you associate with so many other boys, and you can't do that, and wish to please God too, without knowing something of this kind of trial.

M. No, but still, you know, I do think the "persecution" people talk about is rather humbug.

Mrs. H. I think it is too fine a word,—but, on the other hand, to be disliked is hardly pleasanter.

M. Well, for that matter, perhaps it's worse. You'd feel grand and heroic, I suppose, if you were really persecuted, but when it's nothing more than that you can see fellows think you're a fool, it *is* rather trying.

Mrs. H. More than "rather," dear. It is a trial borne for God, which *He* does not think lightly of, depend upon it!"

(Myles had rather a shiny look about the eyes

then, though he was an Eton boy!—but he only remarked,)

"I tell you one thing, Mother—whether we are persecuted, or disliked, it is well to be quite sure that it is 'for righteousness' sake,' and not because of our own priggishness."

Mrs. H. Quite so, Myles—not for our own disagreeable faults and senseless peculiarities.—You see we have found a good many practical lessons from our portion this morning, for though it is so short, it is an immensely important one. The question whether we are really growing in grace cannot be otherwise than important. You know what a sad sight a poor little dwarf is, but an abortive Christian should be considered a far more painful deformity, and a greater proof of the power of Satan in spoiling God's master-work. For God has provided everything for our Growth, and it is a terrible failure if after all we stand still.

Ph. But how can we know that we are growing, Mother?

Mrs. H. Well, I don't say that you can see much difference in your bodily or spiritual stature day by day, or even week by week.

But if we compare ourselves at longer intervals —say a year—with what we were, we ought to find improvement, and we should take it very seriously to heart if we do not. Sin should become more hateful to us, and God's ways pleasanter, and we should get the victory more and more over our besetting sins, and be able more easily to deny ourselves. That is Growth. It is God's Work, and He will carry it on if we don't hinder Him.

We have not yet exhausted the subject of our Master's Mission during those thirty years of what seems like merely waiting, so we will continue it next time. We will pray now,—and then you can run away.

Blessed Lord, Who hast caused all Holy Scriptures to be written for our learning; Grant that we may in such wise hear them, read, mark, learn, and inwardly digest them, that by the nourishment of Thy Holy Word, we may grow up into Thee in all things; till we attain unto the perfect knowledge of the Son of God, unto the full-grown man, unto the measure of the stature of the fulness of Christ. We ask it for His Sake. Amen.

I WANT to be like Jesus,
　So lowly and so meek,
For no one marked an angry word
　That ever heard Him speak.

I want to be like Jesus,
　So frequently in prayer;
Alone upon the mountain top,
　He met His Father there.

I want to be like Jesus:
　I never never find
That He, though persecuted, was
　To any one unkind.

I want to be like Jesus,
　Engaged in doing good,
So that of me it may be said—
　" She hath done what she could."

I want to be like Jesus,
　Who sweetly said to all,—
" Let little children come to Me : "
　I would obey the call.

But oh, I'm not like Jesus,
　As any one may see,
Then, gentle Saviour, send Thy grace,
　And make me like to Thee.
　　　　　WM. M. WHITTEMORE, D.D.

CHAPTER XV.

GOD'S WITNESSES.

JOHN I. 15-18.

MRS. HILLYARD. To-day we continue the subject of our Lord's Mission on earth as "God manifest in the flesh;" and we will read from the 15th to the 18th verse of the 1st chapter of St. John's Gospel, for these verses seem to be the most suitable, and come in order too, as St. John the Baptist's preaching is the next thing recorded in all the Gospels."

These verses Myles read when they had said a few words of prayer.

"John bare witness of Him, and cried, saying, This was He of Whom I spake, He that cometh after me is preferred before me: for He was before me. And of His fulness have all we received, and grace for grace. For the law was given by Moses, grace and truth came by Jesus

Christ. No man hath seen God at any time; the Only Begotten Son Which is in the bosom of the Father, He hath declared Him."

Mrs. H. The first of these verses contains the words of John the Baptist, who as you know was Christ's cousin, and His forerunner. It is doubtful whether the others give us *his* words, or those of the Evangelist who tells the story. The other Evangelists tell us a good deal about John, but what they say of him is of a different character from the account in this Gospel. John's Gospel is indeed altogether unlike the other three. You have noticed that I daresay, Myles—have you, Phyllis?

Phyllis. Yes, I think I have, Mother.

Mrs. H. And what should you say was the difference?

Ph. Well, I hardly know how to put it—but it seems more heavenly.

Mrs. H. Yes, dear, that is just the difference. Jack, can you tell me who John the Evangelist was?

Jack. He was one of the Apostles.

Mrs. H. Do you know anything about him, Elsie?

Elsie. Oh yes! he was the one Jesus loved so much, and who sat with his head on His shoulder at supper time.

Mrs. H. That is quite right; and with such wondrous, blessed intimacy with Jesus, we need not wonder at his writing in a heavenly tone, and as one who had learnt more of the secrets of His Love, and of the deep things of God, than the other Evangelists. His Gospel was not meant to serve the same purpose as theirs, so he supplies what they left untold; and what he tells us of St. John the Baptist was in character with this. John the Baptist was a many-sided man, and whilst Matthew, Mark, and Luke give us one side of his character and teaching, John gives us another, which is the one peculiarly suited to the subject of his Gospel, and therefore I cannot help thinking that the whole of the passage we have read to-day may have been spoken by John the Baptist, although nearly all the commentators attribute to him only the 15th verse. But we are not now concerned with the Baptist's Mission, but with Christ's, and with Christ's during His home-life in Galilee. He was always God's Servant, and this was the time when so much of His real Work was done.—What should you say, children, in a very few words, *was* that Work?

Ph. Always to please God?

Mrs. H. Certainly, but I mean what was His particular Mission on earth as regarded His fellow-men? Why does He when He speaks of Himself, always lay such stress on His being the Sent One of the Father? What was He sent for?

Myles. I think I know what you mean, Mother —He was sent to show God to man.

Mrs. H. Yes, that is what I meant exactly. God sent His Son into the world to *declare Him;* therefore, as I told you before, He is called " the Word." And He fulfilled this Mission at Nazareth as well as afterwards. But as few besides the people in one little Syrian village saw Him during that silent Ministry of His, and as no farther record has been preserved of His Life then than just the few words we have read in Luke's Gospel, one doesn't quite see at first how He could have performed such a tremendously important Mission as manifesting God to mankind. It seems as if the means God had provided for the accomplishment of His purpose had been strangely insufficient. Christ's three years' ministry afterwards don't seem to make up for thirty years of what looks like lost time. Now it is a deeply interesting and important question, and also an intensely practical one— *How was that Mission accomplished?*"

Nobody said anything, so Mrs. Hillyard went on—

"I think this part of our Lord's Work was never finished, in one sense. It was not like the Sacrifice He made upon the Cross. *That* was done once and for ever, and was done by God alone. It was a Work in which we had no part, except indeed that it was our sins which killed Him. * But His Life Mission, though complete as to His part in it, was in fact only to initiate, or begin a Work which was to be carried on after He was gone. It was all His Work, in so far as what He did living and dying secured the ultimate fulfilment of God's great purpose that He should be revealed to man; but He left it to

---

* It would be well to point out to older children that, according to the Levitical Ritual, the slaying of the victim was the work of the offerer, not of the priest.

others to finish it for Him. Of course Jack and Elsie don't understand this, but do you, Myles?

M. No, I can't say I do, for didn't Christ say before He died, "I have finished the Work which Thou gavest Me to do"?

Mrs. H. Yes, but the Work of His Life was to lay a foundation-stone, to make a beginning. He never intended to do more than that Himself.

Ph. Well, but then who was to do the rest?

Mrs. H. Ah, that is just the practical point. *We are.* We are to complete the work which He began of manifesting God to the world.

J. But how, Mother?

Mrs. H. By imitating the way Jesus did it. He began the Work, and we must finish it in the same way—He having left us an Example that we should follow His steps. Now I want each of you to take this *to heart*—even little Elsie—that every Christian is sent into the world by God, as Jesus was, *on a Mission*, or perhaps it would be better to say *with a Commission*, to show people what our Father in Heaven is like, by imitating Jesus.—Tell me, Jack, what is a commission?

J. Oh! I know.

Mrs. H. Tell me then.

J. You sent me to do a commission for you when I took that parcel to Mrs. Thompson.

Mrs. H. Just so. I sent you for that particular thing; and so I sent Myles over to Huxley last night to ask Mr. Green to come to dinner to-morrow. Now suppose you had dropped the parcel into the river, and suppose Myles had never gone near Mr. Green, what sort of commissioners would you have been?

J. Horrid bad ones, of course.

Mrs. H. Well now, dear children, let us all ask ourselves very seriously—*How are we doing our Father's business?* It is just as real, just as definite a work that He has sent you to do for Him, as either of the commissions I gave you. But for fear you should not quite understand me, will each of you three elder ones write down on a bit of paper, in as few words as you can, what this work is exactly that our Heavenly Father has set us."

Myles, Phyllis, and Jack each wrote an answer to this question, and the slips were folded up and given to their mother—then she said—

"Now before I read these I will ask Elsie to tell me the answer to my question, as she can't write well enough. What is it, my sweet one, that God wants you to do for Him?"

E. To let people know that God loves us.

Mrs. H. Yes, darling, that is very nicely said; now we will see what the other answers are — Myles has written "To be Epistles of Christ." Phyllis, "To glorify God." Jack, "To copy Jesus." They are all very good, and I am glad you understood me so well. I think if I had written an answer I should have said—"To be a Witness for God"—a Witness to His Love because He has saved us, as you will see in Isa. xliii. 12. And now, Elsie, what do you think Myles meant by "Epistles of Christ"?

E. I don't know, Mumsey.

Mrs. H. An Epistle is a letter. We ought to be like letters from God to people—letters written by Christ, "known and read of all men." For there are many people, I am sorry to say, who don't care about the Bible, and never read it hardly; and there are many, too, who don't believe it is God's Word; and then again there are multitudes who are so ignorant that they can't read it, and even if they could, would not be able to understand it. To all such people we are sent to *be* a Bible; for they can at least read our lives, and they are quite sure to read them, and to draw their own conclusions as to our characters and motives; and many of them will judge of the God we talk about by the sort of lives we lead. If they see us living pretty much as they do, or perhaps worse—letting our tempers do just what they please with us; or being habitually selfish, or unkind, or greedy, or spiteful, or untruthful, or vain, or money-grubbing; and if, at the same time we profess to have found a Saviour Who will save us from the penalty of our sins; then of course there will be some people who will think that if what we say is true, sin is not of much account in God's sight, and that a little more or less won't matter. We shall be devil's bibles then, for we shall have given them an entirely false notion of God.

Ph. What an awful idea!

Mrs. H. Indeed it is! May God keep us from such iniquity!—and that is only part of the mischief we shall do if we live such lives; for there are others whose own hearts and consciences tell them better than that. They know God must be Good if He exists at all; but yet they don't know how far away everybody has strayed from God, and that only by the Death of Jesus can we be brought back; and *they* will say—"If what these people call 'the Gospel' doesn't make them upright, and kind, and good, we will have nothing to do with it." And they will hate the doctrines of the Cross, more than ever they did, because we have so misrepresented them.—And then again, you must remember the grievous fact, that though we are all God's children, yet an immense number of us sinners have become so utterly estranged from our Father as not to know the least what He is like, or what His feelings are towards us; so that the only feeling of such poor dark souls towards Him is fright. They can't bear to think of Him. He frightens them more, much more, than the thought of ghosts and bogles frightens children whose nurses have been foolish and wicked enough to make them believe in such horrors; because their consciences tell them that they are sinners, and that God "does well to be angry" with them. What we have to show to these poor terrified sinners is just what dear little Elsie said, that though truly God is a Righteous Judge, yet that He is Love, and that He is loving them all the time they are hating the very thought of Him. And we can only do that by being like Him in kindness, and gentleness, and goodness, and unselfishness, and by manifesting in our own conduct that "perfect love" that "casteth out fear."

Ph. Mumsey, what you have been saying about those sort of people who don't know God does so remind me of something that happened the other day. You know that little robin we have been trying to tame? Well, I put some crumbs as usual for him on the window-sill, and he came directly and began to pick them up. I could see him in the glass, but he couldn't see me. So then I thought I *would* make him less afraid of me, and I came quite gently up to the window, and chirped to him—but you should have seen the fright he was in! He was off like a shot. If I had been a tiger he couldn't have been more frightened of me—and I thought if only he could know how I loved him and wanted to kiss him, how surprised he would have been! It made me quite miserable to think that I couldn't make him understand it.

Mrs. H. Thank you so much, dear child, for telling us that little story. Yes, indeed, we are naturally just as ignorant of the Love that is glowing in our Father's Heart. But, Phyllis, you wrote on your slip of paper—" To glorify God." I think I know what made you write that. You were thinking of the question and answer that I have so often told you—that stand at the beginning of the Catechism the children in Scotland learn—were you not?

Ph. Yes, I was.

Mrs. H. Repeat it, will you?

Ph. "What is the chief end of man?—The chief end of man is to glorify God, and to enjoy Him for ever." That is right, isn't it?

Mrs. H. I think it is; but will you explain it to Elsie; I am sure she doesn't understand what the " chief end of man means."

Ph. Doesn't it mean that what God made

everybody for was *that*—that they might glorify Him?

Mrs. H. Yes, but explain what "glorify" means.

Ph. Please Him.

Mrs. H. That is quite right; and it is called "glorify" because as His pleasure is, always Goodness, to do His Will must bring honour to His Name. *He is Worthy* of all Glory, therefore it must be right that He should receive it, and that everything should be working to that End. Nothing else could be right except that: and His Glory, and the happiness of those that love Him, are bound together.

And now we come to what Jack wrote—"To copy Jesus." That is the way to glorify God, by showing in ourselves what He is like; for we must be like God in so far as we are like Christ, Who is "the express Image of His Person." What were you going to say, Myles?

M. I was only thinking that the Old Testament people hadn't a chance of glorifying God in that way, for they couldn't copy Jesus before He was born.

Mrs. H. Of course not! Everybody is bound to glorify God in proportion as they know

Him; and people have always had some dim way of knowing what was right and wrong; thus it was the condemnation of Belshazzar* the Chaldean King, that "the God in whose hand thy breath is, and whose are all thy ways, hast thou not glorified;" and also of the heathen world, that when the things † that God had made had convinced them that "He Is," they had no desire to glorify Him,‡ but rather thrust § away the thought of Him, which was a trouble to them. It had been so from the very first—people would not have God to rule over them, and so they lost their knowledge of Him. Then God chose the family of Abraham to be peculiar witnesses for Him in the midst of the darkened world, but they too fell away, although He did everything that could ‖ be done to teach and bless them. He said of them in a very special way—"This people have I formed for Myself; they shall show forth My praise." ¶ But you know how they failed—how they became "weary" of God —and how at last they killed Jesus, and deter-

---

* Dan. v. 23.   ‡ Rom. i. 21.   ‖ Isa. v. 3, 4.
† Rom. i. 20.   § Rom. i. 28.   ¶ Isa. xliii. 21.

mined that they would not have Him as their King and Saviour; and then God turned * to the Gentiles, and out of them chiefly He raised up His Church. What does that mean, Phyllis?

Ph. The Church? why the people who would have Jesus.

Mrs. H. Yes, and need I say that if the heathens were held responsible for not glorifying God, and if the Jews were called in a more special way to serve Him, that we who have been bought with the precious Blood of Christ, and who know it, and know that therefore we are not our own, are guilty of far worse sin if we do not spend our lives for Him? Don't you see what gross dishonesty it is if we do not?

M. Yes, I suppose it is.

Mrs. H. Say yes, you *know* it is, Myles— don't talk about "supposing." Phyllis said very rightly that the "Church" meant such people † as "would have Jesus"—but would have Him as *what?* We can't have Him as Saviour without having Him as Master too. And indeed it is a very solemn obligation under

---

* Acts xiii. 46. † This need be no contradiction to John xv. 16.

which we placed ourselves when by trusting Him we became members of His Body the Church, for to live for Him has now in a still stronger sense become "our bounden duty and service." I say in a still stronger sense, because everybody who has ever heard of Christ will be judged as a servant * at last. We belong to God because He made us and redeemed us, and therefore He has a right to our services— we can't help ourselves there, nor get rid of the obligation to serve Him however we may wish to do so. But nobody would wish to do so who the least knew what His service was, for it means the only happiness we can have in this world. It is the service of children,† not that of "hired servants,"‡ and it is "perfect freedom." §

M. Of course, Mother, it is all quite true as you put it, and clearly we ought to serve God, but it is a great deal easier said than done. To be really a "faithful servant" seems such a tremendously hard thing.

J. Yes! it doesn't seem possible to be as

---

* Luke xix. 12-26.   ‡ Luke xv. 19.
† Eph. v. 1.   § John viii. 32-36.

good as all that! I am sure I don't know how people can be.

Mrs. H. My darlings, I think you do *know*—we all know where is the Source of strength, and where to go for grace and wisdom. It seems to me that it is altogether a question of whether we *want* to be good; if we do, we shall be. The verses we have read to-day contain the whole secret of *how* we may be good—"Of His Fulness have all we received, and grace for grace." What does "grace" mean, Jack?

J. Does it mean goodness?

Mrs. H. Certainly. "Grace" is *goodness* given freely, and for nothing: so these words merely mean that God is full of Goodness, and will give some of It to any of us who will come to Him for It. In plain English He makes us *good*, bit by bit, just in proportion as we are looking to Him for help. "Grace for grace" might be better rendered "grace upon grace" —fresh grace for every fresh need, just as we require it—given with an unsparing Hand, from the Treasury of all Goodness—from the "unsearchable Riches of Christ."

So you see we don't have to go to work at

our own charges. Our Blessed Lord didn't set us work to do knowing that we couldn't do it, but knowing that we *could*, because He Himself supplies the power. He is not like the Egyptian task-masters who said, "Go and make the full tale of bricks, and find your own straw!"—then, indeed, we might have sat down in despair; but He gives us all that is needful for the task He sets us; even when that task seems such an impossible one as to be His representatives on earth; or, as I said before, His "witnesses."

M. That is a grand Mission, certainly.

Mrs. H. Indeed it is! I have dwelt particularly on it to-day, as Christ's "declaring" God, and John the Baptist again "bearing witness" to Him, has been our subject. And yet even the desire to be a witness for God should not be our chief motive in wishing and trying to be good; for that is, after all, only a consequence. If we are like Christ, we shall, as a matter of course, shine for Him, and draw others to Him. But *to do right for Righteousness' own sake, is the grand first principle,* though we don't perhaps feel that at first; but our Father leads us on to see and feel it more and more, as we grow in likeness to Him. Can you understand this, Myles?

M. I think I can, just a little.

Mrs. H. I will try and explain it more fully. When we first come to Jesus, and believe that He has saved us, and given Himself for us, gratitude for our own deliverance, and love to Him Who died for us, are our strongest motives for serving God. That is indeed a loving and obedient, but it can hardly be called an intelligent service. But if we go on faithfully obeying God we shall become more like Him, and shall be led more and more to see and feel the value of Goodness for its own sake, and to love God* *most* because He is Good, "giving thanks at the remembrance of His Holiness," and rejoicing that there is in Him an untainted, and an unfailing Source of Perfect Righteousness; that He Himself is, in fact, the Impersonation of all Goodness and Truth. Do you understand me now?

---

* 2 Chron. v. 13, vi. 41, vii. 3; Ps. vii. 17, xlv. 6, 7, xcix. 5, c. 4, 5, cvi. 1-3, cvii. 1, cxlv. 7; Prov. xi. 23; Isa. xi. 5, xxiii. 5, 6; Eph. v. 9.

M. I believe I do.

Mrs. H. I think even children ought to feel, in a measure, the greatness and grandness of *Right*, and the thorough badness of *Wrong*. St. Paul felt this very strongly when he told the Corinthians,* "we pray to God that ye do no evil ; not that we should appear approved, *but that ye should do that which is honest*, though we be as reprobates." And it was not only his own reputation as an Apostle that he seemed to treat so lightly ; he had not forgotten the "injury," as we should say, that their evil living would do to the cause of Christ —but yet he adds, " For we can do nothing against the truth, but for the truth."

Ph. I don't understand that the least, Mother, though I think I understood what you said before.

Mrs. H. I think you will understand this too, dear, if you think a little, for it only means that Paul knew that the Lord can take care of His own Truth, and that we can't really injure His Cause, for it is not the poor fragile thing we

---

* 2 Cor. xiii. 7, 8.

sometimes think it. We may safely leave it in His Hands, although He condescends to work by us. It is often a great comfort to remember that. And now there is just one thing more I want to say, though we ought to stop.—I wish you to notice the distinction drawn in the 17th verse, "The law was *given* by Moses, but grace and truth *came* by Jesus Christ." In the one case God *gave* His Law on a mount that burned with fire, and amid blackness and darkness and tempest, and with a Voice so terrible that they which heard It entreated that It might not speak to them any more. He gave it too through a sinner, who himself was so unable to keep it that in the very act of carrying the written tables down the mountain, he flung them to the ground in a passion. —But in the other case God didn't send. He *came* Himself. His holy and righteous Law *came*—not enforced by terrors, but personified in the Lamb of God—in the sweet teachable Child of Nazareth—in the bravest, kindest, noblest Man that ever lived; Who loved little children, and never frightened them, and only wanted to make them good and safe and happy.

You can see at once in what a far more responsible position such a Revelation of God places *us* than the Jews in Old Testament times.

Ph. Yes, of course it must.

Mrs. H. We have long exceeded our time, and must close now, but I trust we may all remember, even little Elsie, that every day the Commission we each of us have to do for our Father is to be good, and so to witness for Him —to go forth and let it be seen that "for me to live is Christ."

O God, the Father of Lights, in Whom is no darkness at all, grant that by the Light of the Sun of Righteousness, we may walk without stumbling, and thus shine brightly for Thee in a world still darkened by sin, to the Glory of Thy Name. We ask it for His Sake. Amen.

THE "FAITHFUL WITNESS IN HEAVEN."

Ps. lxxxix. 37.

Long since upon those distant hills
  The Sun's last rays were cast,
The glory of the western sky
  Has died away at last.

Yet not in darkness are we left
  For up in heaven, so bright,
The Moon shines calmly, whilst she floods
  The sleeping world with light.

The centuries are passing on,
  And still the Moon is fair,
Still she walks worthy of the Name
  He gave Who set her there.

A "faithful witness" to the Sun,
  His glory she displays
Gazing on him "with open face,"
  And shining in his rays.

Her lustre shed on flower and leaf,
  On meadow, wood, and stream,
A strange entrancing beauty gives,
  Surpassing poet's dream.

And thus she draws our hearts above
  To realms beyond the sky,
Where Beauty dwells, and Light, and Love,
  To all Eternity.

And shall not we who by His Grace
 Know Jesus as the Lord,
Jesus, "the Sun of Righteousness,"
 Transmit His Rays abroad?

Shall not His followers on the earth,
 Whose ways His Feet have trod,
Learn from the faithful Moon to bear
 True witness unto God?

Catching some splendour from His Beams,
 Drawing some hearts above,
Making some frightened sinners feel
 Quite sure that "GOD is LOVE."

CONCLUSION.

OUR TEACHER.

JOHN XIV. 16, 17; XV. 26; XVI. 13-15; 2 TIM. III. 14-17.

WE can follow the Hillyards no farther in their Bible Readings. They now entered upon the public Ministry of our Blessed Lord, when He went about teaching, and preaching, and doing good. They would then come to the End of that Perfect Life, and read how He laid It down—"the Just for the unjust, that He might bring us to God:"—how His Body was then laid in the grave, from which He so soon rose Victorious to comfort the hearts of His brethren, and in a few weeks to ascend in great triumph to His Father's Kingdom in Heaven. Nor would they stop there. They would go on to read of the Descent of the Holy Ghost, Who came in fulfilment of Christ's promise to take His Place on earth, gathering together His disciples, and thus building up His Church. They would study, too, the Acts of these first Christians, as well as the letters written to their various assemblies, or to individuals amongst them, by the teachers whom God had " set over " them ;—perhaps even learning some lessons from the wonderful and mysterious book which closes the New Testament with a Cry from Earth to Heaven that Jesus would take unto Him His great Power and reign.

But we need follow them no farther. Why should we ? We too have our Bible, and One ready and waiting to teach us to understand it, and to "guide us into all truth." Let us wait upon Him, and then amidst the confusion of many and various human teachers, we need never be led astray, but may profitably, and humbly, and thankfully learn from them all. But if what we learn about God is *merely* "taught by the precept of men"—never mind what grand names they may call themselves by—it will be very little good to us, for we shall find numbers of good people, and clever people,

OUR TEACHER. 277

all telling us different things about religion, and all equally certain they are right. So that if we have no more sure guide than they can be, we shall always be in perplexity, and at last perhaps be led by the one that speaks the most positively, or else believe none of them, which will be worse still, as all of them can teach us much truth. That would be like drifting about in a boat on the sea, without rudder or compass.

No! if we really want to know the truth about God, and how best to please Him, and how to keep straight on our course amidst the waves and storms of this troublesome world, we must remember that the Holy Ghost is the only Teacher Who can never go wrong, and that He is a Real Person, here on this earth on purpose to teach us through His Word—just as really here (though we can't see Him) as Jesus was— and that He is quite sure to teach us if we pray to God expecting to be taught by Him.

But many people, I am afraid, both old and young, don't the least wish to learn about God, and think they could be quite happy without Him, if only they could get what they like here.

If the Conversations in this little book may

lead any one with such foolish, bad thoughts as that, to see that God is worth caring about, and bring them to repentance, and then straight to the Father Who is loving them so much, what a blessing it will be!

And if we who do know that God is Love, and Light, and Goodness, may be brought to a determination that by His Help we will show everybody round us how Good He is, by reflecting His Character in some degree, that will be a greater blessing still, because "living" books teach ever so much better than printed ones, and can win many more souls to God.

NOTE.

Three plagiarisms are thankfully acknowledged :—

1. The connection between the texts standing at the head of Chapter 1 was learnt from the late Mr. Brownlow North, who has given great prominence to the subject of that chapter in some of his writings.

2. One or two thoughts on the Loss of Jesus, expressed in a sermon by the Rev. W. Aitken, have been reproduced from memory, with more or less accuracy, on p. 199.

3. As have also some thoughts on the character of Christ's miracles, contained in "The Perfect Man," by the Rev. Harry Jones, on p. 219.

APPENDIX.

" BUT whatever the boy Jesus may have learned as child or boy in the house of His mother, or in the school of the synagogue, we know that His best teaching was derived from immediate insight into His Father's will. . . . Written on His inmost spirit, written on His most trivial experiences, written in sunbeams, written in the light of stars, He read everywhere His Father's Name. . . . We know how from every incident [of daily life at Nazareth] the games of its innocent children, the buying and selling in its little market-place, the springing of its perennial fountain, the glory of its mountain lilies in their transitory loveliness, the hoarse cry in their wind-rocked nest of the raven's callow brood—He drew food for moral illustration and spiritual thought.

" Nor must we lose sight of the fact that it was in these silent, unrecorded years that a great part of His work was done. . . . In these years He 'began to do' long before He 'began to teach.' They were the years of a sinless Childhood, a sinless Boyhood, a sinless Youth, a sinless Manhood, spent in that humility, toil, obscurity, submission, contentment, prayer, to make them an eternal example to all our race. . . . The legends of early Christianity tell us that night and day, where Jesus moved and Jesus slept, the cloud of light shone round about Him. And so it was; but that light was no visible Shechinah; it was the beauty of holiness; it was the peace of God."

. . . .

" It has been implied that there are but two spots in Palestine where we may feel an absolute moral certainty that the Feet of Christ have trod, namely—the well-side at Shechem, and the turning of that road from Bethany over the Mount of Olives from which Jerusalem first bursts upon the view. But to these I would add at least another—the summit of the hill on which Nazareth is built. That summit is now unhappily marked, not by any Christian monument, but by the wretched, ruinous, crumbling *wely* of some obscure Mohammedan saint. Certainly there is no child of ten years old in Nazareth now, however dull and unimpressionable he may be, who has not often wandered up to it; and certainly there could have been no boy at Nazareth in olden days who had not followed the common instinct of humanity by climbing up those thymy hill-slopes to the lovely and easily accessible spot which gives a view of the world beyond. The hill rises six hundred feet above the level of the sea. Four or five hundred feet below lies the happy valley. The view from this spot would in any country be regarded as extraordinarily rich and lovely; but it receives a yet more indescribable charm from our belief that here, with His feet among the mountain flowers, and the soft breeze lifting His hair from His temples, Jesus must often have watched the eagles poised in the cloudless blue, and have gazed upwards as He heard overhead the rushing plumes of the long line of pelicans, as they winged their way from the streams of Kishon to the Lake of Galilee. And what a vision would be outspread before Him, as He sat at springtime on the green and thyme-besprinkled turf! To Him every field and fig-tree, every palm and garden, every house and synagogue, would have been a familiar object; and most fondly of all amongst the square flat-roofed houses would His eye single out the little dwelling-place of the village carpenter."

. . . .

" The outward life of Jesus was the life of all those of His age, and station, and place of birth. He lived as lived the other children of peasant parents in that quiet town, and in a great measure as they live now. He who has seen the children of Nazareth in their red caftans, and bright tunics of silk or cloth, girded with a many-coloured sash, and sometimes covered with a loose outer jacket of white or blue—he who has watched them at their games, and heard their ringing laughter as they wander about the hills of their little native vale, or play in bands on the hillside beside their sweet and abundant fountain, may perhaps form some conception of how Jesus looked and played when He too was a Child. And the traveller who has followed any of those children—as I have done—to their simple homes, and seen the scanty furniture, the plain but sweet and wholesome food, the uneventful, happy patriarchal life, may form a vivid conception of the manner in which Jesus lived. Nothing can be plainer than those houses, with the doves sunning themselves on the white roofs, and the vines wreathing about them. The mats, or carpets, are laid loose along the walls ; shoes and sandals are taken off at the threshold ; from the centre hangs a lamp which forms the only ornament of the room ; in some recess in the wall is placed the wooden chest, painted with bright colours, which contains the books or other possessions of the family ; on a ledge that runs round the wall,' within easy reach, are neatly rolled up the gay-coloured quilts, which serve as beds, and on the same ledge are ranged the earthen vessels for daily use ; near the door stand the large common water-jugs of red clay with a few twigs and green leaves—often of aromatic shrubs—thrust into their orifices to keep the water cool. At meal-time a painted wooden stool is placed in the centre of the apartment, a large tray is put upon it, and in the middle of the tray stands the dish of rice and meat, or *libbân*, or stewed fruits, from which all help themselves in common. Both before and after the meal the servant, or the youngest member of the family, pours water over the hands from a brazen ewer into a brazen bowl. So quiet, so simple, so humble, so uneventful was the outward life of the family at Nazareth.

.   .   .   .   .   .

"Yet this poverty was not pauperism; there was nothing in it either miserable or abject ; it was sweet, simple, contented, happy, even joyous. Mary, like others of her rank, would spin, and cook food, and go to buy fruit, and

evening by evening visit the fountain, still called after her 'The Virgin's Fountain,' with her pitcher of earthenware carried on her shoulder or her head. Jesus would play, and learn, and help His parents in their daily tasks, and visit the synagogues on the Sabbath days."
Farrar's " Life of Christ,"
Vol. I., pp. 61-63, 92-95, 100, 101.

THE END.

PRINTED BY BALLANTYNE, HANSON AND CO
EDINBURGH AND LONDON

THE GOLDEN LADDER SERIES.

Uniform in size and binding, with Coloured Illustrations.

Crown 8vo, cloth.

1. THE GOLDEN LADDER: Stories Illustrative of the Eight Beatitudes. By SUSAN and ANNA WARNER. 3s. 6d.
2. THE WIDE WIDE WORLD. By SUSAN WARNER. 3s. 6d.
3. QUEECHY. By the same. 3s. 6d.
4. MELBOURNE HOUSE. By the same. 3s. 6d.
5. DAISY. By the same. 3s. 6d.
6. THE OLD HELMET. By the same. 3s. 6d.
7. THE THREE LITTLE SPADES. By ANNA WARNER. 2s. 6d.
8. NETTIE'S MISSION: Stories Illustrative of the Lord's Prayer. By ALICE GRAY. 3s. 6d.
9. DAISY IN THE FIELD. By SUSAN WARNER. 3s. 6d.
10. STEPPING HEAVENWARD. By Mrs PRENTISS. 2s. 6d.
11. WHAT SHE COULD, AND OPPORTUNITIES. Tales. By SUSAN WARNER. 3s. 6d.
12. GLEN LUNA. By ANNA WARNER. 3s. 6d.
13. DRAYTON HALL. Stories Illustrative of the Beatitudes. By ALICE GRAY. 3s. 6d.
14. WITHOUT AND WITHIN: A New England Story. 3s. 6d.
15. VINEGAR HILL STORIES. Illustrative of the Parable of the Sower. By ANNA WARNER. 3s. 6d.
16. LITTLE SUNBEAMS. By J. H. MATTHEWS. 3s. 6d.
17. THE HOUSE IN TOWN, AND TRADING. 3s. 6d.
18. DARE TO DO RIGHT. By the Author of "Nettie's Mission." 3s. 6d.
19. SCEPTRES AND CROWNS AND THE FLAG OF TRUCE. Tales. By the Author of "The Wide Wide World." 3s. 6d.
20. URBANÉ AND HIS FRIENDS. By the Author of "Stepping Heavenward." 2s. 6d.
21. HOLDEN WITH THE CORDS. By the Author of "Without and Within." 3s. 6d.
22. GIVING TRUST: Containing "Bread and Oranges," and "The Rapids of Niagara." Tales Illustrating "The Lord's Prayer. By SUSAN WARNER. 3s. 6d.
23. GIVING HONOUR: Containing "The Little Camp on Eagle Hill," and "Willow Brook." By the Author of "The Wide Wide World," &c. 3s. 6d.

THE EIGHTEENPENNY JUVENILE SERIES.

Uniform in size and binding, 16mo, Illustrations, cloth.

1. AUNT EDITH ; or, Love to God the Best Motive.
2. SUSY'S SACRIFICE. By the Author of "Nettie's Mission."
3. KENNETH FORBES ; or, Fourteen Ways of Studying the Bible.
4. LILIES OF THE VALLEY, and other Tales.
5. CLARA STANLEY ; or, A Summer among the Hills.
6. THE CHILDREN OF BLACKBERRY HOLLOW. By ANNA WARNER.
7. HERBERT PERCY ; or, From Christmas to Easter.
8. PASSING CLOUDS ; or, Love Conquering Evil.
9. DAYBREAK ; or, Right Struggling and Triumphant.
10. WARFARE AND WORK ; or, Life's Progress.
11. EVELYN GREY. By the Author of " Clara Stanley."
12. THE HISTORY OF THE GRAVELYN FAMILY.
13. DONALD FRASER.
14. THE SAFE COMPASS, AND HOW IT POINTS. By the Rev. R. NEWTON, D.D.
15. THE KING'S HIGHWAY ; or, Illustrations of the Commandments. By the same.
16. BESSIE AT THE SEASIDE. By JOANNA H. MATTHEWS.
17. CASPER. By the Author of " Dollars and Cents," &c.
18. KARL KRINKEN ; or The Christmas Stocking. By SUSAN and ANNA WARNER.
19. MR RUTHERFORD'S CHILDREN. By the Author of " Dollars and Cents."
20. SYBIL AND CHRYSSA. By the same.
21. HARD MAPLE. By the same.
22. OUR SCHOOL-DAYS. By C. S. H.
23. AUNT MILDRED'S LEGACY. By the Author of "The Best Cheer," &c.
24. MAGGIE AND BESSIE, AND THEIR WAY TO DO GOOD. By JOANNA H. MATTHEWS.

EIGHTEENPENNY JUVENILE SERIES—*continued.*

25. GRACE BUXTON; or, The Light of Home. By EMMA MARSHALL.
26. LITTLE KATY AND JOLLY JIM. By ALICE GRAY.
27. BESSIE AT SCHOOL. By JOANNA H. MATTHEWS.
28. BESSIE AND HER FRIENDS. By the same.
29. BESSIE IN THE MOUNTAINS. By the same.
30. HILDA AND HILDEBRAND; or, The Twins of Ferndale Abbey.
31. GLEN ISLA. By Mrs DRUMMOND.
32. LUCY SEYMOUR; or, "It is more blessed to Give than to Receive." By the same.
33. LOUISA MORETON; or, "Children, obey your Parents in all Things" By the same.
34. THE WILMOT FAMILY; or, "They that deal truly are His Delight." By the same.
35. SOWING IN TEARS AND REAPING IN JOY. By FRANZ HOFFMANN. Translated from the German by Mrs Faber.
36. BESSIE ON HER TRAVELS. By JOANNA H. MATTHEWS.
37. LITTLE NELLIE; or, The Clockmaker's Daughter.
38. THREE LITTLE SISTERS. By Mrs MARSHALL.
39. MABEL GRANT. A Highland Story.
40. THE RETURN FROM INDIA. By the Author of "Hilda and Hildebrand."
41. THE COURT AND THE KILN: A Story Founded on the Church Catechism.
42. SILVER SANDS; or, Pennie's Romance. By Miss CRAMPTON.
43. LIONEL ST CLAIR. By L. A. MONCREIFF, Author of "Herbert Percy."
44. THE KNOTS TOM GILLIES TIED AND UNTIED. By Mrs G. GLADSTONE.
45. THE LITTLE PREACHER. By the Author of "Stepping Heavenward," &c.
46. LOVE FULFILLING THE LAW.
47. ANTOINE THE ITALIAN BOY. By the Rev. C. W. DENISON.
48. TWO LITTLE HEARTS. By SOPHIE SPICER.
49. DICK'S FIRST SCHOOL-DAYS. By Mrs H. BARNARD.
50. THREE LITTLE BROTHERS. By Mrs MARSHALL.

THE
ONE SHILLING JUVENILE SERIES.
Uniform in size and binding, 16mo, Illustrations, each 1s., cloth.

1. CHANGES UPON CHURCH BELLS. By C. S. H.
2. GONZALEZ AND HIS WAKING DREAMS. By C. S. H
3. DAISY BRIGHT. By EMMA MARSHALL.
4. HELEN; or, Temper and its Consequences. By Mrs G. GLADSTONE.
5. THE CAPTAIN'S STORY. By W. S. MARTIN.
6. THE LITTLE PEAT-CUTTERS. By EMMA MARSHALL.
7. LITTLE CROWNS, AND HOW TO WIN THEM. By the Rev. J. A. COLLIER.
8. CHINA AND ITS PEOPLE. By a MISSIONARY'S WIFE.
9. TEDDY'S DREAM; or, A Little Sweep's Mission.
10. ELDER PARK; or, Scenes in our Garden. By Mrs ALFRED PAYNE, Author of "Nature's Wonders," &c.
11. HOME LIFE AT GREYSTONE LODGE. By the Author of "Agnes Falconer."
12. THE PEMBERTON FAMILY, and other Stories.
13. CHRISTMAS AT SUNBURY DALE. By W. B. B.
14. PRIMROSE; or The Bells of Old Effingham. By Mrs MARSHALL.
15. THE BOY GUARDIAN. By C. E. BOWEN.
16. VIOLET'S IDOL. By JOANNA H. MATTHEWS.
17. FRANK GORDON. By Author of "The Young Marooners;" and LITTLE JACK. By Author of "The Golden Ladder."
18. THE COTTAGE ON THE CREEK. By the Hon. Mrs CLIFFORD-BUTLER.
19. THE WILD BELLS, AND WHAT THEY RANG. By W. S. MARTIN. Edited by C. S. HARINGTON.
20. TO-DAY AND YESTERDAY. By Mrs MARSHALL.
21. GLASTONBURY; or, The Early British Christians. By Mrs ALFRED PAYNE.
22. MAX: A Story of the Oberstein Forest.
23. MARY TRELAWNY. By CHRISTIAN REDFORD.
24. LUPICINE; or, The Hermit of St Loup.
25. LOVING-KINDNESS; or, The Ashdown Flower Show.
26. BETWEEN THE CLIFFS. By Mrs MARSHALL.
27. FRITZ; or, The Struggles of a Young Life.

THE SELECT SERIES.

Crown 8vo, each 3s. 6d. cloth. Bound by BURN. Most of them with Illustrations.

1. DERRY: A Tale of the Revolution. By CHARLOTTE ELIZABETH.
2. THE LAND OF THE FORUM AND THE VATICAN. By NEWMAN HALL, LL.B.
3. THE LISTENER. By CAROLINE FRY.
4. DAYS AND NIGHTS IN THE EAST; or, Illustrations of Bible Scenes. By HORATIUS BONAR, D.D. Illustrations.
5. THE HOLY WAR. By JOHN BUNYAN. Coloured Illustrations
6. THE PILGRIM'S PROGRESS. By JOHN BUNYAN. Coloured Illustrations.
7. THE MOUNTAINS OF THE BIBLE: Their Scenes and their Lessons. By the Rev. JOHN MACFARLANE, LL.D.
8. HOME AND FOREIGN SERVICE; or, Pictures in Active Christian Life.
9. LIFE: A Series of Illustrations of the Divine Wisdom in the Forms, Structures, and Instincts of Animals. By P. H. GOSSE, F.R.S.
10. LAND AND SEA. By P. H. GOSSE, F.R.S.
11. JOHN KNOX AND HIS TIMES. By the Author of "The Story of Martin Luther."
12. HOME IN THE HOLY LAND. By Mrs FINN.
13. A THIRD YEAR IN JERUSALEM: A Tale Illustrating Incidents and Customs in Modern Jerusalem. By the same.
14 and 15. THE ROMANCE OF NATURAL HISTORY. By P. H. GOSSE, F.R.S. First and Second Series.
16. BLOOMFIELD: A Tale. By ELIZABETH WARREN, Author of "John Knox and his Times," &c.
17. TALES FROM ALSACE; or, Scenes and Portraits from Life in the Days of the Reformation, as Drawn from Old Chronicles. Translated from the German.
18. HYMNS OF THE CHURCH MILITANT. Edited by the Author of "Dollars and Cents," &c.
19. THE PHYSICIAN'S DAUGHTERS; or, The Spring-Time of Woman. A Tale.
20. WANDERING HOMES AND THEIR INFLUENCES. By the Author of "The Physician's Daughters."
21. THE INGLISES; or, How the Way Opened. By the Author of "Christie Redfern's Troubles."
22. LOWENCESTER: A Tale. By SYDNEY HAMPTEN.

T

BOOKS FOR THE YOUNG.
BY THE REV. J. R. MACDUFF, D.D.

1. FOOTSTEPS OF ST PAUL. Being a Life of the Apostle. Designed for Youth. With Illustrations. Thirty-first Thousand, crown 8vo, 5s. cloth.
2. THE STORY OF BETHLEHEM. With Illustrations by THOMAS. Eighth Thousand, crown 8vo, 2s. 6d. cloth.
3. THE EXILES OF LUCERNA; or, The Sufferings of the Waldenses during the Persecution of 1686. Fourth Thousand, small crown 8vo, 2s. 6d. cloth.
4. THE WOODCUTTER OF LEBANON. Seventh Thousand, 16mo, 2s. cloth.
5. THE GREAT JOURNEY: A Pilgrimage through the Valley of Tears to Mount Zion, the City of the Living God. Sixth Thousand, 16mo, 1s. 6d. cloth.
6. THE CITIES OF REFUGE; or, The Name of Jesus. A Sunday Book. Tenth Thousand, 16mo, 1s. 6d. cloth.
7. THE LITTLE CHILD'S BOOK OF DIVINITY; or, Grandmamma's Stories about Bible Doctrines. Fourteenth Thousand, 16mo, 1s. cloth limp.
8. WILLOWS BY THE WATERCOURSES; or, God's Promises to the Young. A Text Book. Eighth Thousand, 64mo, 3d. sewed, 6d. cloth limp.
9. TALES OF THE WARRIOR JUDGES. A Sunday Book for Boys. Third Thousand, small crown 8vo, 2s. 6d. cloth, with Illustrations.

LITTLE BOOKS FOR LITTLE PEOPLE.
Royal 16mo, Illustrations, cloth.

1. LITTLE SUSY'S SIX BIRTHDAYS, LITTLE SERVANTS AND SIX TEACHERS. 2s. 6d.
2. PLEASANT PATHS FOR LITTLE FEET. By the Rev. J A. COLLIER. 2s. 6d.
3. LITTLE LOU'S SAYINGS AND DOINGS. By the Author of "Little Susy." 3s. 6d.
4. LITTLE THREADS; or, Tangle Thread, Silver Thread, and Golden Thread. By the Author of "Little Susy." 2s. 6d.
5. EFFIE'S YEAR: A Tale for the Little Children of the Church. 2s. 6d.
6. LITTLE ELSIE'S SUMMER AT MALVERN. By the Hon. Mrs CLIFFORD BUTLER. 2s. 6d.
7. GETTING WELL: Tales for Little Convalescents. By Mrs S. H. BRADFORD and others. 2s. 6d.

BALLANTYNE'S MISCELLANY
OF ENTERTAINING AND INSTRUCTIVE TALES.
16mo, Illustrations, each 1s., cloth.
Or, in sets, with handsome cloth box, price 17s. 6d.

1. FIGHTING THE WHALES; or, Doings and Dangers on a Fishing Cruise.
2. AWAY IN THE WILDERNESS; or, Life among the Red Indians and Fur Traders of North America.
3. FAST IN THE ICE; or, Adventures in the Polar Regions.
4. CHASING THE SUN; or, Rambles in Norway.
5. SUNK AT SEA; or, The Adventures of Wandering Will in the Pacific.
6. LOST IN THE FOREST; or, Wandering Will in South America.
7. OVER THE ROCKY MOUNTAINS; or, Wandering Will in the Land of the Redskin.
8. SAVED BY THE LIFE-BOAT; or, A Tale of Wreck and Rescue on the Coast.
9. THE CANNIBAL ISLANDS; or, Captain Cook's Adventures in the South Seas.
10. HUNTING THE LIONS; or, The Land of the Negro.
11. DIGGING FOR GOLD; or, Adventures in California.
12. UP IN THE CLOUDS; or, Balloon Voyages.
13. THE BATTLE AND THE BREEZE; or, The Fights and Fancies of a British Tar.
14. THE PIONEERS: A Tale of the Western Wilderness.
15. THE STORY OF THE ROCK.
16. WRECKED, BUT NOT RUINED.

Also, price 3s. 6d. each,

I.
TALES OF ADVENTURE ON THE SEA. Containing Nos. 1, 3, 9, and 13 of "Ballantyne's Miscellany."

II.
TALES OF ADVENTURE BY FLOOD, FIELD, AND MOUN-TAIN. Containing Nos. 5, 6, 7, and 11 of "Ballantyne's Miscellany."

III.
TALES OF ADVENTURE; or, Wild Work in Strange Places. Containing Nos. 2, 10, 12, and 14 of "Ballantyne's Miscellany."

IV.
TALES OF ADVENTURE ON THE COAST Containing Nos. 4, 8, 15, and 16 of "Ballantyne's Miscellany."

WORKS BY R. M. BALLANTYNE.

Crown 8vo, each 5s. cloth, with Illustrations.

NEW VOLUME.

UNDER THE WAVES; or, Diving in Deep Waters.

1. RIVERS OF ICE: A Tale Illustrative of Alpine Adventures and Glacier Action.
2. THE PIRATE CITY. An Algerine Tale.
3. BLACK IVORY: A Tale of Adventure among the Slavers of the East Coast of Africa.
4. THE NORSEMEN IN THE WEST; or, America before Columbus.
5. THE IRON HORSE; or, Life on the Line. A Railway Tale.
6. THE FLOATING LIGHT OF THE GOODWIN SANDS. A Tale.
7. ERLING THE BOLD: A Tale of the North Sea-Kings.
8. DEEP DOWN: A Tale of the Cornish Mines.
9. FIGHTING THE FLAMES: A Tale of the London Fire-Brigade.
10. SHIFTING WINDS: A Tough Yarn.
11. THE LIGHTHOUSE; or, The Story of a Great Fight between Man and the Sea.
12. THE LIFEBOAT: A Tale of our Coast Heroes.
13. GASCOYNE, THE SANDALWOOD TRADER. A Tale of the Pacific.
14. THE GOLDEN DREAM: A Tale of the Diggings.

LONDON: JAMES NISBET & CO., 21 BERNERS STREET.

RECENTLY PUBLISHED.

I.

Crown 8vo, 7s. 6d. cloth,

THE ROMANCE OF MISSIONS;

Or, Inside Views of Life and Labour in the Land of Ararat. By MARIA A. WEST, Missionary of the American Board in Turkey. With an Introduction by Mrs. CHARLES, Author of "The Schonberg Family."

II.

Post 8vo, 7s. 6d. cloth,

FORTY YEARS' MISSION WORK IN POLYNESIA AND NEW GUINEA.

From 1835 to 1875. By the Rev. A. W. MURRAY, London Missionary Society. With Illustrations.

III.

Crown 8vo, 3s. 6d. cloth,

OUR COFFEE ROOM.

By ELIZABETH R. COTTON. With Preface by Lieut.-General Sir ARTHUR COTTON, R.E., K.C.S.I.

IV.

Crown 8vo, 3s. 6d. cloth,

MEMORIALS OF A QUIET MINISTRY;

Being the Life and Letters of Rev. ANDREW MILROY. By his Son, the Rev. ANDREW WALLACE MILROY, M.A., Oxon. With Portrait and Illustrations.

V.

Post 8vo, 5s. cloth,

CONVERSATIONS ON THE GOSPEL ACCORDING TO ST LUKE.

By EMILY TEMPLE FRERE.

VI.

Crown 8vo, 2s. 6d. cloth; 3s. gilt edges,

THE GOSPEL AND ITS MINISTRY.

By ROBERT ANDERSON, LL.D.

VII.
4to, 21s. cloth,
WILD FLOWERS OF THE HOLY LAND.
Fifty-four Plates, printed in colours. Drawn and Pointed after Nature by HANNAH ZELLER, Nazareth. With a Preface by the Rev. H. B. TRISTRAM, Canon of Durham, and an Introduction by EDWARD ATKINSON, Esq., F.L.S., F.Z.S.

VIII.
16mo, 2s. cloth,.
THE GATES OF PRAISE,
And other Original Hymns, Poems, and Fragments of Verse. By the Rev. J. R. MACDUFF, D.D., Author of "The Gates of Prayer," "Morning and Night Watches," &c.

IX.
Crown 8vo, 3s. 6d. cloth,
SOUTH AFRICAN MISSIONS.
By C. H. MALAN, Author of "A Soldier's Experience of God's Love."

X.
New and Enlarged Edition, crown 8vo, 5s. cloth,
ILLUSTRATIVE TEXTS AND TEXTS ILLUSTRATED.
By the Rev. J. W. BARDSLEY, M.A., Vicar of St. Paul's, Greenwich.

XI.
Crown 8vo, 3s. 6d. cloth,
WYCH HAZEL:
A Tale. By SUSAN and ANNA WARNER, Authors of "The Wide, Wide World," &c.

XII.
Crown 8vo, 5s. cloth,
IMMANUEL'S LAND,
And other Pieces. By A. R. C.

XIII.
Crown 8vo, 3s. 6d. cloth,
FOUNDATION TRUTHS:
Lectures on Romans viii. 33, 34, preached in Portman Chapel during Lent 1875. By the Rev. J. W. REEVE, M.A., Canon of Bristol, Author of "The Titles of Jehovah," &c.

XIV.
Crown 8vo, 5s. cloth,
RIVERS OF ICE.
A Tale Illustrative of Alpine Adventure and Glacier Action. By R. M. BALLANTYNE, Author of "The Pirate City." With Illustrations.

XV.
Crown 8vo, 3s. 6d. cloth,
GIVING TRUST:
Containing "Bread and Oranges," and "The Rapids of Niagara." Tales illustrating "The Lord's Prayer." By SUSAN WARNER. With Coloured Illustrations. Golden Ladder Series.

XVI.
Royal 32mo, 1s. 6d. cloth, gilt edges,
THE BORDER LAND, AND OTHER POEMS.
By L. N. R., Author of "The Book and its Story."

XVII.
Crown 8vo, 4s. 6d. cloth,
ECHOES FROM A CONTINENTAL CITY AND A LONDON SUBURB.
By the Rev. F. J. SERJEANT, Vicar of St Mary's, Fulham. New Edition, Enlarged.

XVIII.
Crown 8vo, 1s. 6d. cloth,
INSTRUCTIONS ON THE CHURCH CATECHISM:
Being Fifty-two Lessons for Bible Class, Sunday School, &c. By the Rev. ROWLEY HILL, M.A., Vicar of Sheffield, Author of "The Titles of our Lord."

XIX.
Crown 8vo, 3s. 6d. cloth,
SEEKING THE LOST.
Incidents and Sketches of Christian Work in London. By the Rev. C. J. WHITMORE, Author of "The Bible in the Workshop."

XX.
Crown 8vo, 2s. 6d. cloth,
THE GOSPEL IN SANTHALISTAN.
By an Old Indian. With Preface by the Rev. H. BONAR, D.D.

XXI.
Crown 8vo, 3s. 6d. cloth,
HOLDEN WITH THE CORDS.
By the Author of "Within and Without." With Coloured Illustrations. Golden Ladder Series.

XXII.
Post 8vo, 7s. 6d. cloth,
TWELVE MONTHS IN MADAGASCAR.
By the Rev. J. MULLENS, D.D., Foreign Secretary of the London Missionary Society. With Illustrations.

XXIII.
Crown 8vo, 3s. 6d. cloth,
THE SAINTLY CALLING.
By the Rev. C. D. BELL, M.A., Rector of Cheltenham, and Hon. Canon of Carlisle.

XXIV.
Crown 8vo, 3s. cloth,
THE WOMEN OF INDIA AND CHRISTIAN WORK IN THE ZENANA.
By Mrs WEITBRECHT.

XXV.
Crown 8vo, 5s. cloth,
CLEFTS OF THE ROCK;
Or, The Believer's Grounds of Confidence in Christ. By the Rev. J. R. MACDUFF, D.D., Author of "The Gates of Prayer," &c.

XXVI.
Crown 8vo, 3s. cloth,
THE RENT VEIL.
By the Rev. HORATIUS BONAR, D.D., Author of "Christ of God," &c.

XXVII.
4to, 10s. 6d. cloth,
EDDA:
Tales of a Grandmother. A History of Denmark. Edited by PHILOJUVENIS. New Edition. With many Illustrations.

XXVIII.
Crown 8vo, 5s. cloth,
THE PIRATE CITY:
An Algerine Tale. By R. M. BALLANTYNE, Author of "Black Ivory," &c. With Illustrations.

www.ingramcontent.com/pod-product-compliance
Lightning Source LLC
Chambersburg PA
CBHW030812230426
43667CB00008B/1171